Have fun cooking +
eating your way through
this book!

All the best

Nick

My Daddy Cooks

About the author

Thanks to his parents, Nick Coffer has been eating fresh, tasty meals all his life, but his real love affair with food began when he lived in France in his twenties. After the recession led him to wind down his drinks' distribution company, Nick became a stay-at-home dad, looking after his toddler, Archie. In 2009 he launched MyDaddyCooks.com, the hugely successful video blog, which shows Nick and his son cooking together in their tiny kitchen in Watford. Nick presents a weekly food and drink programme on BBC Three Counties radio, and lives with Archie, baby Matilda and his wife Jo. *My Daddy Cooks* is his first book.

Praise for MyDaddyCooks.com

'Cooked this on Tuesday, absolutely scrumptious.'
Noileum on Turbo-quick Shepherd's Pie

'I've never made a risotto in my life before and have just made this – how easy??? And yummy.'
Samsmumlou on Oven-baked Risotto

'Oh Man... this chicken hotpot is absolutely 5 stars!!! I have tried most of your recipes and all of them are big success! Yum...yum...'
Eva on Chicken and Tarragon Hotpot

'I cooked this yesterday and it tasted fantastic. Thank you so much for posting such lovely, easy to cook recipes.'
Josephine on Easy Chicken and Apricot Casserole

'Made this slab of absolute deliciousness this morning.'
Janine on No-bake Chocolate Tiffin Cakes

'Yum!!! This cake is delicious and it's true that it is even better the day after... Thank you!'
Sylvie on Muddy Flourless Chocolate Cake

To Jo and Archie

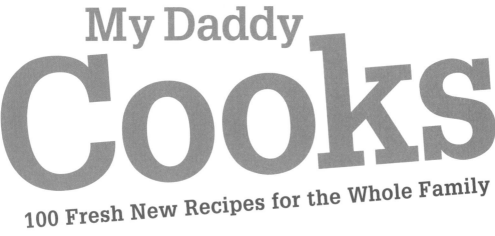

My Daddy Cooks

100 Fresh New Recipes for the Whole Family

NICK COFFER

HODDER &
STOUGHTON

Contents

Nick

Archie

Introduction

If there had been more room on the front cover, a suitable title for this book might have been *My Daddy Cooks – or how to cook delicious and easy family meals, in the tiniest kitchen, even with the chaotic and messy intervention of a toddler.*

If you have watched any of the videos on my blog of Archie and me cooking together, you will know exactly what I am referring to. And yet, even when all the cake mixture ends up halfway down Archie's sleeves, or when half a pot of oregano finds its way into the lamb stew, we still make fresh food that tastes delicious.

The reality is that home cooking should not be about following complicated recipes. It's not about fancy preparation, presentation and ingredients that may not be available in the local shop. It's about serving up great, easy food, which the whole family can enjoy.

I call it 'Tuesday evening cooking'.

You know, midweek, busy, tired cooking. Cooking that is not going to be unduly affected if you use 50g less flour for a cake, or double the quantities of cumin in a curry or marinate some meat for 2 minutes instead of 24 hours. All the recipes on the blog, and in this book, meet those most important of criteria – they are foolproof and toddlerproof. There is not a single ingredient in this book that will ruin a dish if you don't follow the exact quantities and most recipes here wouldn't even be diminished by missing out the odd ingredient.

Not only do I feel that this is the way home cooking should be, it is also a realistic necessity if you do have a little helper in the kitchen with you. Have you ever tried convincing a small child about how much a 'pinch' of a spice actually is, or persuading them that beef stock is not the FIRST ingredient to go in the frying pan when making a Bolognese sauce?!

Of course, you don't have to have any kids in the kitchen with you to make these recipes. And it goes without saying that you don't even have to be a dad. But as they have all been road-tested in the toughest kitchen environment – a tiny three metres square kitchen with my little toddler in tow – you can be confident that they are all extremely cookable and will provide you and your family with lovely meals.

So what are we cooking?

All the recipes, be they old classics or new twists, are cooked in the same My Daddy Cooks style as on the blog:

Preparation is always quick, fun and easy. There is plenty of scope for mixing, throwing, splashing, rolling and bashing. Even the dishes that require longer cooking, such as the stews, require little or no intervention once the dish is prepared. Lots of corners are cut and fancy techniques go out of the window – but the finished product is always just as good. This is not the book to use if you want to learn how to make foams; there is no blanching, basting or julienning; and you will more than happily survive without steamers, mandolins, pizza stones and all manner of other specialist kitchen equipment.

Everything is home made. None of the recipes in this book use store-bought sauces. Not only does the finished product never taste as fresh, I am not even sure using these sauces actually reduces cooking time. As an example, making the Thai green curry paste in this book could not be quicker and you just wouldn't get the same flavours from a jar. And anyway, you hardly need to buy a cookbook to learn how to use ready-made ingredients. My only concession to this is using ready-made puff and filo pastries in the recipes, but I know very few people who would make their own in the midst of busy family life.

All ingredients are easily available. All these recipes pass the supermarket test. Unless you are really unlucky with the choice at your local shops and supermarkets, there won't be any need to use specialist retailers or food merchants to cook anything in this book. Hunting down ingredients is hardly conducive to easy cooking.

None of the food I cook, either on the blog or in this book, is specifically conceived to be 'child-friendly'. This is not a children's cookbook, no more than it is a book of children's food. The recipes don't 'hide' fruit and vegetables, I don't sweeten sauces, I don't avoid strong flavours or interesting textures. We have tried to let Archie experience a diverse spread of flavours from the very earliest days. This has meant that he has

developed his own strong preferences, which he displays in a typically feisty and direct manner. He certainly doesn't eat everything we offer him. Far from it. There are loads of things he doesn't like and, as with any wilful toddler, if the wind changes direction, he can suddenly decide that a flavour or ingredient is just not for him anymore. But he does have a curiosity around food – and the ingredients that make up a dish – and it is this curiosity that means I continue to cook with variety. If he doesn't like something, I don't label him as fussy. He is just being like any adult – showing what he likes and doesn't like (albeit usually more forcefully than we would!)

Also, I would hate for anyone to get the impression that every single mealtime in our house is a culinary adventure of discovery. We couldn't survive without store-bought hummus; we would be lost without fish fingers; I dread to think what we would do without simply cooking eggs in their various forms; and we love getting a takeaway in too.

So this is not a book telling you to cook fresh three times a day, every day. That certainly doesn't happen in my own house, so I wouldn't expect it to happen anywhere else either. When we get a takeaway in though, it's because we all really fancy one and will enjoy it. It's not usually because time is short. There are loads of recipes in this book that can be prepared and cooked in less time than it takes to call in a takeaway (including, appropriately, an incredibly fast and fresh home-made pizza), so lack of time needn't be the reason behind not cooking fresh food at home.

A note about salt. As this book has food in it to be eaten by kids and adults alike, I have not left salt out of the ingredients. When Archie was very little, we did not add salt to food we cooked, but we did still happily use ingredients such as soy sauce. As he grew older, we used more salt in our cooking. This book is not about telling you whether you should use salt or not, and how much you should use. Although most of the recipes use it, I would recommend using as much or as little as you want, at your own discretion.

Before the book and the blog

My love of good, fresh food goes all the way back to my childhood. My mum was (and remains) a great cook and always tried to put something tasty on the table, even in the periods when the household finances could barely cope. It's only when I grew up that I learnt that things got so bad at certain times that my mum used to feed me and my sister and then eat toast with my dad when he came back from work. He was a pretty accomplished cook too and taught me everything I know about being messy in the kitchen.

I moved to France when I was 18 (to live with my French teacher, but that is another story) and it was there that I really learnt about cooking and eating fresh food, prepared simply. I was also taken by the table culture there. It is no secret that French family life – and, indeed, life in general – revolves around eating together and I loved this about the country. This culture no doubt influenced the way I have always tried to ensure we eat together as a family since Archie was old enough to sit in a highchair.

I returned to the UK and launched a business in 2003, supplying restaurants and hotels with premium drinks. By spring 2009, the business was 6 years old but, as the recession hit, things went downhill very fast. Worse still, I had the future of a little one-year-old toddler to worry about. I became a stay-at-home dad almost by default, while my wife, Jo, continued to work part-time as a school counsellor and private psychotherapist.

Eating ice cream with my granddad

I often say that this period was both the best and worst of my life. Terrible for the rut I found myself in, but at the same time amazing because it enabled me to spend real quality time around my little boy. Time that I knew could never be repeated or replaced if I wasn't there for it. As most parents would say, with kids 'you blink and you miss it,' and here I was, with a grandstand view of these precious moments.

The kitchen was the perfect place for Archie and me to entertain each other. I had always been a very good cook and Archie loved spending time with me in there. Sometimes to help cook, other times just to potter about, do water play in the sink or create his own concoctions in a bowl.

It didn't matter what he did. All that mattered was that we were having fun together. I had to be in the kitchen anyway to prepare our food and it was a lovely added bonus that this time didn't just disappear as 'dead time' with no interaction with Archie.

By the autumn of 2009, I still hadn't found a new route, professionally speaking. I had the idea to blog about our experiences in the kitchen as no more than a means to just get some creative focus on something, but I realised that merely writing about it would not suffice. You needed to be there to understand it! So I decided to film us, even though I had absolutely no experience of filming or editing and our kitchen was too small to swing even a proverbial cat in.

And yet, the blog was born. I quietly posted the first few videos (which were terrible!) and, to my astonishment, we had a worldwide following within a matter of weeks. I was at the centre of the kind of internet story I had previously only read about.

We found ourselves on *BBC News*, on the radio – and Archie managed to appear on the front page of the *London Evening Standard*. As the ultimate irony, the one project I had started without any view whatsoever to it becoming a job had in fact spawned a brand new career all of its own.

In the kitchen

The great thing about the blog is that none of the videos are planned or contrived; they simply document what happens in the kitchen. And I do really love being in the kitchen with Archie. They are wonderful moments of quality time spent together. But does he really cook? The answer is both yes and no. Most importantly, it doesn't actually matter at all. It is just about us hanging out, having fun and him being engaged with what goes into getting food on the table.

He was actually in the kitchen with me from an early age. I think that from 6 months old, he was either hanging off my hip or sitting precariously on the worktop – neither of which I would advocate! At around 14 months old, we bought him a special kitchen stand called a FunPod and, by the time he started appearing on blog videos, he had already been getting used to the kitchen for a year. We started with lots of cold cooking and this is still my preferred activity with him in the kitchen. That's why many of the recipes in this book require no heat at all in order to be prepared, apart from maybe putting the dish in the oven.

If you do decide to let your kids into the kitchen – and I hope that this book will inspire you to do so – how would I recommend you go about it? Obviously much depends on the actual age of the children involved, but I have learnt that, first and foremost, I have to leave any mess inhibitions at the kitchen door. If there is flour to drop, milk to spill, oil to drip or water to splash, Archie will happily oblige. But it is all part of the fun and anything can be easily cleaned in a kitchen.

I also have to forget about perfection. Things go horribly wrong when Archie is around. That's why all the recipes in this book have been devised to survive even the most catastrophic interventions.

With Archie's limited concentration span, I try to prepare as many of the ingredients as possible before he joins me and it is impossible to cook things that require long waits between stages. For this reason, home-made pastry is impossible because he just wouldn't have the patience to wait for it to chill first, then cook blind, and then cook with a filling. In fact, I wouldn't have the patience either, so we make a good team!

Even so, I have somehow learnt to stay calm and keep communicating with him. Even if I look relaxed on the videos, I am being hypervigilant. The only thing that stops Archie turning the kitchen from a messy-zone

to a war-zone is me not getting annoyed or stressed. With heat hazards in the kitchen, staying calm and clear-headed is vital, as is constantly talking to him. I never assume he has understood something and I am more than happy to repeat the same thing over and again. If he is working on a chopping board near a hot dish, I will repeatedly and calmly remind him of the danger nearby.

The kitchen is a great place for children to learn to listen to instructions, to understand dangers and to communicate. Not to mention the early maths, early science and even early geography that come into the mix too. This is why it was pointed out to me by a regular visitor to my blog, who is an infant school teacher, that cooking is so brilliant for kids because it is one of the only activities that covers every element of the Early Years curriculum. Archie is learning so much in the kitchen and he doesn't even realise it.

As this book is 100 per cent a cookbook and not a children's activity book, I have deliberately steered clear of specifying what parts of the recipes kids may or may not enjoy helping with. I haven't even stated what parts of the recipes Archie enjoys doing because that changes by the day too. All the recipes are packed from start to finish with elements your children can help with if they want to. Much will depend on the age of the children you have with you in the kitchen, what they enjoy doing and what you are comfortable letting them do. I just like to think of Archie as a willing sous-chef, available nearby to help if he wants to. Some days he will be keen to help all the way from the fridge to the frying pan. On others, he will just as happily pass me ingredients and chop away at a mushroom while I cook. This means that I am equally happy having him in the kitchen with me if I am cooking a stir-fry in a hot wok or if we are cold-cooking my no-bake chocolate tiffin cake.

At the shops

Having Archie engaged in the cooking process actually starts in the shops for us. I really enjoy shopping with Archie. I am often asked whether I plan my meals – and my shopping – meticulously. I would love to say that I do, but sadly it would be far from the truth. I really admire people who are organised enough in their heads to do it but whenever I have tried to sit down and write a meal plan it just hasn't worked for me.

That said, I don't shop randomly.

So what do I do? Well, firstly I make sure that my fridge, freezer and cupboards are always stocked with more or less the same basic ingredients, which I use repeatedly in my cooking. You will see these ingredients turning up over and again in my recipes and I list them on page 22. What's more, they pretty much all have a long shelf-, fridge- or freezer-life and I know that I can always put together a quick and tasty meal using just these basic ingredients if needs be.

As for meat, fish and vegetables, I am certainly not going to say that you have to buy everything organically from farm shops and fishmongers! This is not that kind of book and, anyway, I love my local supermarkets and enjoy the quality, variety and value for money of produce there. But I am also lucky to have a fishmonger within walking distance and, every couple of months, I fill a drawer in my freezer with fish. I do the same with my meat too. Again, I am lucky to have two butchers nearby, where the meat is great value and Archie enjoys coming up to the counter and choosing with me. I tend not to buy chicken portions, preferring instead to buy a whole chicken and cut it up. That may sound a chore, but I posted a video on the blog showing how quick and easy it is to do, and so much cheaper.

With the fridge, freezer and cupboards full of these primary and secondary ingredients, all that remains is to decide what we fancy eating, work out how much or how little time I have available and choose the recipe accordingly. It is not a perfect system, but I never completely run out of ingredients and my flexible, throw-it-all-in approach to cooking means I never have any wastage either. Any fresh ingredient that looks on its last legs quickly finds its way into a stir-fry, a pasta or a frittata in my kitchen.

Time to cook

If there is one theme that I have tried to maintain through this whole book, it is making food fun – all the way from the shop to the table – for you and your family. This is most definitely not a parenting book, nor is it a book about how to get children to eat. It's just a simple family cookbook, chock-full of delicious, easy and fresh recipes, which experienced cooks will enjoy making and less confident cooks will have no problems at all mastering.

I really hope you and your family enjoy cooking – and of course eating – your way together through this book and that it gives you loads of ideas for brightening up your mealtimes and getting your kids involved in the kitchen – while having lots of fun in the process!

Nick

Inside my cupboards

Here is the list of staple ingredients I always make sure I have to hand.

Cupboards

Baking powder

Balsamic vinegar

Basmati rice

Bicarbonate of soda

Breadcrumbs or matzo meal

Caster or golden caster sugar

Chilli pepper

Chinese five spice powder

Cinnamon sticks

Coconut milk

Curry powder

Dried oregano

Filo pastry

Garam masala

Garlic powder

Golden syrup

Ground cinnamon

Ground coriander

Ground cumin

Honey

Icing sugar

Ketchup

Maple syrup

Olive oil

Paprika

Pastas of various shapes and sizes

Plain flour

Powdered vegetable stock

Risotto rice

Self-raising flour

Sesame oil

Soft brown sugar

Soy sauce

Thai fish sauce

Tinned tomatoes

Turmeric

Vanilla extract

Vegetable oil

White wine vinegar

Worcester sauce

Fridge

Crème fraîche

Fresh ginger

Fresh Parmesan cheese

Garlic

Large eggs

Ready-made puff pastry

Strong Cheddar

Tomato purée

Freezer

Chipolatas

Chorizo

Frozen berries

Frozen peas

Pancetta/streaky bacon

Pitta

1
Beyond Toast

Archie often wakes up wanting to play immediately and, where time permits (particularly at the weekend), he loves to come and help in the kitchen. Of course we eat lots of simple toast, cereals and eggs in the morning. But we also like to be a bit creative too on occasion and these fun-to-make breakfasts and brunches will add some variety, even for the busiest kids.

Fruity popovers

I find it impossible to resist Yorkshire puddings, so making the sweeter equivalent for breakfast seems like an excellent idea to me. Popovers are slightly lighter than Yorkshire puddings, thanks to the added butter, but there is not much in it. You can find special popover tins, which are basically tall and narrow muffin tins, but these popovers will work in a normal large muffin tin without any problem. I serve mine with fresh red fruits and a large dollop of strawberry or raspberry jam, but butter, honey or golden syrup also work brilliantly.

Muffin tins vary in size, but this mix will make 12 popovers in one or two muffin tins.

Preheat your oven to 230°C/450°F/Gas Mark 8.

1 Grease each individual muffin cup generously using a pastry brush – or some kitchen paper – dipped in vegetable oil.
2 Put the muffin tins in the preheated oven for 5 minutes.
3 While the tins are in the oven, melt the butter in a non-metallic bowl in the microwave on full power for 60 seconds (or in a pan on the hob) and leave to cool for a minute or two.
4 Mix together the eggs, milk, melted butter and vanilla extract, and then whisk in the flour and sugar. You want the mixture to be free of lumps, but try not to whisk it too frenetically.
5 Cut a slice of butter into twelve pea-sized cubes. Take the muffin tins out of the oven and drop a piece of butter into each cup.
6 Put the tins back in the oven for about 30–40 seconds, then take them out of the oven and half fill each individual cup with the batter (make sure the oven door is closed to keep the heat in).
7 Cook the popovers in the oven for 18 to 20 minutes. Resist ALL temptations you – or anyone else! – may have to open the oven door until after at least 18 minutes. Doing so will result in failed popovers!
8 The popovers are ready when they are beautifully risen and golden. Serve immediately, dusted with a little icing sugar for added effect, with the condiments of your choice.

Serves 4

Preparation time 10 minutes

Cooking time 20 minutes

2 tablespoons butter, plus a slice for the tins

4 large eggs

250ml milk

A drop of vanilla extract

140g plain flour

2 tablespoons caster sugar

Icing sugar, to dust (optional)

Jam and fresh red fruits, to serve

Breakfast pikelets with blueberries and maple syrup

'Bluebellies', as Archie called them for so long, have always been a favourite in this house and they go perfectly with these breakfast pikelets (think pancakes, but thicker). I reckon they are almost as quick to make as hot porridge and, because the morning is no time to be getting scales and measures out of your cupboards, I have given easy tablespoon measures here. And even if you miscount or lose the fight over the flour and the spoon (a frequent occurrence in our kitchen), these pikelets will not go wrong. Short of pouring only milk into a frying pan, almost any combination of flour, eggs and milk will produce something tasty for your breakfast.

This mix will make approximately 20 pikelets. They freeze without problem and can be reheated for 15 seconds in a microwave or in a warm frying pan with a little butter.

1 Melt the butter in a non-metallic bowl in the microwave on full power for 30 to 40 seconds (or in a pan on the hob).
2 Mix together the flour, sugar and cinnamon.
3 Whisk in the egg.
4 You need the mix to be moderately thick, but lump-free, so whisk in three-quarters of the milk and check the consistency. If the mix still looks way too thick, add the rest of the milk.
5 Add the melted butter.
6 Heat up a large frying pan on a medium heat. You want the pan to be hot, but not smoking.
7 While the pan is heating up, pour the syrup and the blueberries into a saucepan and heat gently. Keep an eye on them, you just want them to warm through.
8 Drop ½ teaspoon butter into the heated frying pan and shake the pan so the butter covers the whole base.
9 Drop the mix in large tablespoonfuls straight into the pan. So as not to crowd the pan, cook in batches.
10 As soon as the pikelets start to bubble, turn them over and cook on the other side for a few minutes until golden brown.
11 Remove the pikelets from the pan and repeat stages 8-10 until they have all been cooked.
12 Pile two or three pancakes on to each plate, spoon over the syrup and top with a dollop of crème fraîche.

Serves 4 (with a few pikelets left over)

Preparation time 5–10 minutes

Cooking time 10–15 minutes

1 tablespoon butter, plus extra for cooking with

7 heaped tablespoons self-raising flour

1 tablespoon caster sugar

A sprinkling of ground cinnamon

1 egg

A tall glass of milk (approximately 200ml)

4 tablespoons maple syrup

200g punnet of blueberries

Crème fraîche, to serve (optional)

Oven-baked French toast

Of course, French toast is a breakfast staple and appears regularly in cookbooks, but I find it can sometimes be somewhat, well, splatty when frying it in a pan, and this is not always ideal if a little helper is in the kitchen. This version bakes the bread, which takes a little longer, but it is just as tasty as the traditional frying method and, if anything, the bread actually crisps up a little more.

Preheat your oven to 220ºC/425ºF/Gas Mark 7.

1 Mix together the eggs, the milk and the vanilla extract.
2 Put the slices of bread in the egg mixture and leave the liquid to absorb for a few minutes on both sides.
3 Very generously grease a non-stick baking tray with butter. Cook the bread in the oven for 15 minutes, turning the slices over after about 10 minutes.
4 Leave the slices to cool down a bit. They are likely to have puffed up a little in the oven, but will deflate while they cool.
5 Serve the toasts warm – with your choice of jams, marmalade, syrup or honey.

Serves 4

Preparation time 5–10 minutes

Cooking time 15 minutes

4 eggs

200ml milk

A little dash of vanilla extract

1 medium baguette, cut diagonally into 2cm thick slices

Baked eggs in ham cups

Here's a fun twist on your morning eggs. These baked eggs are less heavy than fried eggs, less unpredictable than poached eggs and make a pleasant change from scrambled eggs. They are extremely easy and fun to assemble and look delicious sitting in their bespoke ham cups, which crisp up nicely in the oven. The added cheese and cherry tomatoes make this dish a really filling and satisfying start to any day.

Preheat your oven to 180°C/350°F/Gas Mark 4.

1 Grease the ramekins with butter.
2 Put one slice of ham in each ramekin and press it gently against the base and sides to create a little 'ham cup'.
3 Crack an egg into each ramekin.
4 Drop a couple of cubes of cheese and two halves of tomato either side of each egg yolk. Season with a little salt and pepper to taste.
5 Bake in the oven for 12 minutes. Check the egg to see if the egg whites have set firm and the yolks are still soft. If they are not quite ready, put them back in the oven for a few minutes.
6 Take the ramekins out of the oven, leave to cool for a few moments and carefully remove the ham cups. Serve with toast and butter.

Serves 4

Preparation time 10 minutes

Cooking time 12–15 minutes

You will need four ramekins

4 large slices of ham (not too thick or else they will be hard to set in the ramekins)

4 large eggs

8 small (1cm) cubes of Cheddar or any hard cheese of your choice

4 cherry tomatoes, cut in half

Salt and freshly ground black pepper

Full-English breakfast frittata

The vegetable frittata on My Daddy Cooks has always been one of the most popular recipes on the blog. Frittatas are great for using up whatever fresh produce you may have in the fridge and they are cooked very differently to omelettes. With omelettes the key is heat and speed, whereas frittatas are cooked more slowly and finished off under the grill. This is a breakfast, or even brunch, version and the ingredients are very much interchangeable.

Preheat your oven's grill to high.

1 Break the eggs into a large bowl, pour in the milk and lightly beat everything together. Season the mix and add in the thyme if you have some to hand.
2 Pour a good drizzle of oil into a large, non-stick frying pan on a medium heat and fry the sausages until they are browned and cooked. If you are using the large sausages, you will need to take them out of the pan and cut them into chunks once they are done.
3 Throw in the mushrooms and cook for a minute, then add the tomatoes and cooked potatoes and carry on cooking for a further minute.
4 Pour in the egg mixture, let it seep around the other ingredients and leave it to cook gently for 7 to 8 minutes. You don't need to stir the eggs once they are in the pan.
5 Once the frittata is well set underneath and nearly set on top, put it under the grill for 3 to 4 minutes so that it becomes golden and fluffy. If you don't have a grill, you can put the pan in a hot oven instead.
6 Let the frittata cool slightly, then turn it out, upside down, on to a large plate. Slice it up and eat it straight away – with some hot baked beans for good measure!

Serves 4 (with some probably left over)

Preparation time 10 minutes

Cooking time 20 minutes

8 eggs

3–4 tablespoons milk

Salt and freshly ground black pepper

A pinch of thyme leaves (optional)

Olive oil

6 chipolatas (or 4 large pork sausages)

2 small handfuls of button mushrooms, cut in half

12 cherry tomatoes

A couple of handfuls of leftover roast potatoes or cooked new potatoes (skin off), chopped into smallish chunks

1 tin of baked beans, to serve (optional)

Fruit compote, yoghurt and granola glasses

This fruit compote makes a syrupy and pleasant change from simply adding fruit to yoghurt in the morning. Dried fruit lends itself particularly well to this kind of quick poaching and the result is lovely fruity goodness – stacked with granola and yoghurt – to start the day with. Although it is relatively quick to prepare, the compote can be made the night before and kept in the fridge. It will also last a few days in an airtight container. If you don't like prunes, you can simply double the quantity of apricots.

1 In a saucepan, heat up 400ml water, the sugar and cinnamon stick until the sugar dissolves and the liquid starts to bubble.
2 Add the pear pieces and dried fruit and simmer on a medium heat for 5 to 7 minutes until the fruit is tender.
3 Take the compote off the heat, remove the cinnamon stick and leave it to cool down for at least 10 minutes.
4 Take four glasses and spoon equal quantities of cooked fruit into each.
5 Pour some yoghurt on top of the fruit and finish off with a handful of granola.

Serves 4

Preparation time 5 minutes
(plus time to cool down)

Cooking time 7 minutes

2 tablespoons soft brown sugar

A small cinnamon stick
(or ½ a large one)

2 barely ripe pears (if they are too soft, they will break up during cooking), peeled, cored and cut into big chunks

250g ready-to-eat dried apricots

250g ready-to-eat prunes

150ml plain thick yoghurt

4 handfuls of granola

Savoury breakfast bread pudding

I can't tell you how much I love this dish! Not quite a quiche, not quite a soufflé, not quite 'eggy' bread, the breakfast bread pudding is possibly a mix of all three. It is pure family comfort food, a 100 per cent make ahead dish (it needs overnight chilling) that is ideal for lazy brunches. In America, these savoury bread puddings are called 'stratas', meaning layers, and are a Christmas morning staple. The great thing about this is that once you have the base of bread, eggs and milk, you can fill the pudding with pretty well anything savoury that takes your fancy.

1 Grease the dish well with butter.
2 Add a little olive oil to a hot pan and fry the bacon until it starts to go crispy and golden. Add the mushrooms and continue to cook until slightly golden.
3 Add all the spinach leaves and keep stirring while they cook down (or 'melt', as Archie likes to say).
4 Leave the bacon, mushrooms and spinach to cool down a little. If they get mixed with the egg while still hot, the egg will start to cook.
5 Meanwhile, spread the bread cubes evenly over the base of the dish then sprinkle the grated Cheddar over the top.
6 Mix the eggs with the milk and crème fraîche. Season, adjusting salt according to the saltiness of the bacon.
7 Pour the egg mixture over the bread.
8 Sprinkle the cooked ingredients evenly over the eggs and bread and fold them in to the mix.
9 Press down on the ingredients to make sure everything is mixed in well (this is Archie's favourite part!)
10 Cover the dish with clingfilm and put a heavy weight (such as a good cookbook) on top to compress all the ingredients. Leave to chill in a fridge (including the book!) for at least 8 hours and preferably overnight.
11 Take the dish out at least 30 minutes before cooking. Preheat the oven to 180°C/350°F/Gas Mark 4. Cook for 1 hour covering with foil if the top overbrowns.
12 The savoury bread pudding will rise like a soufflé and sink when you take it out of the oven. Leave to settle for 5 minutes. Serve warm.

This easily serves 6 people for brunch

Preparation time 20–25 minutes (plus overnight chilling)

Cooking time 1 hour 10 minutes

You will need a deep 12 inch (30cm) baking dish

Olive oil

250g unsmoked bacon, cut into strips

125g chestnut mushrooms, sliced finely

150g fresh spinach (or three blocks of frozen spinach, defrosted)

1 stale large, crusty baguette (the crustier and more flavoursome the better), cut into 2.5cm cubes

250g extra-mature Cheddar cheese, grated

10 large eggs

675ml semi-skimmed milk

200ml half-fat crème fraîche

Salt and freshly ground black pepper

Griddled foil bananas

These bananas take just a few moments longer to prepare than it takes to actually peel them and the parcels can easily be assembled the night before, left in the fridge and cooked in the morning. The butter and sugar caramelise during cooking and the bananas come out perfectly soft. Served with some citrus fruit, this is an all-in-one breakfast fruit salad in a parcel.

1 Butter each sheet of aluminium foil, taking great care not to tear it.
2 Peel the bananas. Cut them lengthways and lay two halves on each of the aluminium foil sheets.
3 Sprinkle the mint and soft brown sugar over the bananas, then drizzle the orange juice and a squirt of lemon juice over them.
4 Wrap up the bananas tightly and snugly by bringing the four sides of each aluminium foil sheet towards the top and scrunching the sides together.
5 Heat a griddle pan or a heavy-based frying pan on a high heat until it is hot.
6 Turn the heat down to medium and simply place the banana parcels into the pan, being careful not to tear the aluminium foil.
7 Cook for 10 minutes, then remove carefully from the pan and leave to cool for a few minutes before opening the parcels (there will be a gush of steam, so be vigilant).
8 Serve in the foil parcels with the orange and grapefruit pieces.

Serves 4

Preparation time 5 minutes

Cooking time 10 minutes

You will need four sheets of aluminium foil, approximately 30 x 20cm

1 tablespoon butter

4 ripe (but not falling apart) bananas

4 tablespoons soft brown sugar

8 tablespoons orange juice

Juice of 1 lemon

4 sprigs of mint

Segments of orange and grapefruit, to serve

Golden banana cake

The two things that can be very off-putting about banana cake are its dull colour and the fact that it can be quite dry and stodgy. This recipe solves both those problems. The use of dark soft brown sugar gives the cake a lovely golden colour and the addition of some oil and sultanas makes it very light, moist and fluffy. The oil also helps to prolong the life of the cake and it will sit happily in an airtight container for up to 3 days. The texture is somewhere between a cake and a loaf and we love serving this at breakfast.

Preheat your oven to 180°C/350°F/Gas Mark 4.

1 Grease the loaf tin (if it is not a non-stick pan, line the base and sides with baking parchment and grease the parchment too.)
2 Sieve together the flour, the baking powder and the bicarbonate of soda into a bowl.
3 Beat together the butter and sugar until light and creamy, then mix in the mashed bananas and the sultanas.
4 Add in the flour and the eggs alternately, about one third of each at a time. Give the mix a good stir after each addition to make sure everything is evenly mixed in.
5 Stir in the oil, pour the cake mix into the tin and smooth over the top.
6 Put the tin in the middle of your oven and bake for 1 hour.
7 Test whether the cake is ready by inserting a skewer into it. If it comes out dry, the cake is ready. If you find that your cake needs a little longer to cook through, simply cover it with a little aluminiun foil to stop it burning on top. Even when it seems to be going too brown on top, this cake doesn't dry out on the outsides. If anything, it benefits from a darker crust.
8 When the cake is ready, leave it to cool for 5 minutes in the tin, then turn it out on to a work surface or a wire rack to cool further. The cake is at its finest when still warm, but will last for 2 or 3 days in an airtight container.

Preparation time 15 minutes

Cooking time 1 hour

You will need a 2lb (900g) loaf tin

300g plain flour

2 teaspoons baking powder

½ teaspoon bicarbonate of soda

150g butter

150g dark soft brown sugar

2 very ripe large bananas (the older, browner and riper the better), mashed

80g sultanas or raisins

2 eggs

100ml vegetable oil

2
Lighter Bites

I didn't want to simply call this chapter 'Lunch' because it's not quite a lunch chapter in the conventional sense. I just think of these recipes as being lighter than full meals. Some are quick lunch bites for the week, others require a little more time and I save them for the weekend. Nearly all of them work brilliantly as light suppers too and some of them, such as the muffins, are great any time of the day!

Feta and cream cheese filo tart (spanakopita)

The Greeks call this 'spanakopita' – by far my favourite name for any dish – and versions of this filo tart exist all through the Balkans and Turkey. Making this tart is akin to arts and crafts in the kitchen for kids because the filo sheets need to be individually brushed with melted butter and carefully stacked. That said, it is extremely easy to make and a big favourite in our house. Although best served warm, this tart is a lovely cold picnic treat too.

Preheat your oven to 180°C/350°F/Gas Mark 4.

1 Mix together the two cheeses in a bowl until relatively smooth. Stir in the eggs, then the parsley and dill and season well with salt and pepper.
2 Melt the butter in a non-metallic bowl in the microwave on full power for 40 seconds (or in a pan on the hob). Mix in the olive oil.
3 Generously brush the dish with the butter/oil mixture.
4 Take one sheet of filo pastry. You want to trim it so it is just a little bit bigger than your baking dish. (This will probably mean cutting it in half widthways). Cover up the remaining sheets with a moist kitchen cloth so they do not dry up. Put one of the halves into the dish. You'll probably need to scrunch down the edges so that it lies flat. Generously brush with the butter mixture, then place the other half of the sheet on top and, again, brush generously with the butter mixture.
5 Spread a thin layer of the cheese mixture all over the filo.
6 Take another sheet of pastry, cut it in half again and layer the two halves on top of the cheese mixture, brushing each sheet generously with the butter mixture.
7 Continue to alternate two buttered halves of a filo pastry sheet with a layer of the cheese mixture until the cheese mixture runs out. You will probably get three layers of cheese.
8 Put two final layers of filo pastry on top of the last layer of cheese, brushing both generously with the butter, and prick the surface a little with a fork.
9 Bake in the oven for 30 minutes. The tart will rise and will be golden on top when it's ready.

Serves 6 for lunch
(or 4 for supper)

Preparation time 15–20 minutes

Cooking time 30 minutes

You will need a 30 x 20cm baking dish

400g feta cheese (it's worth getting the barrel-aged feta if you can find it)

200g soft cream cheese

2 eggs

A big handful of flat-leaf parsley leaves, chopped

A small handful of dill, chopped

Salt and freshly ground black pepper

125g butter

125ml olive oil

1 pack of filo pastry (available in all supermarkets)

You can happily add some spinach to the cheese mix too. Simply defrost 3 blocks of frozen spinach and squeeze out all the water before mixing it together with the cheese.

Pan bagnat (traditional French tuna sandwich)

Pan bagnat literally means 'wet bread' in local dialect in Nice and it is a fitting description of this delicious take on a classic sandwich. The bread is fairly well soaked in olive oil, filled with all the classic ingredients of a Niçoise salad, flattened and left to rest for an hour or so while all the flavours mature. Originally a hearty fisherman's lunch, these sandwiches are a true taste of the South of France and a perfect lunch. Traditionally made using round country bread rolls, they work just as well with an extra crispy baguette.

You can also use cooked broad beans, radishes and artichoke hearts. Personally, I love adding a few anchovies too.

1 Cut the baguette in half lengthways, making sure the bottom half is thicker than the top half. Pick out some of the bread. You don't want to completely empty the baguette by any stretch. You just want to make a little room for the ingredients.
2 Lay both halves of the baguette crust side down. Cut the garlic clove in half and rub it all over the inside of the baguette. Drizzle lots of olive oil over the bread (you want more than a light trickle, but less than a drenching) and then lightly drizzle over some white wine vinegar.
3 Stack the vegetable ingredients and the egg on to the bottom half of the baguette, add the olives and crumble the tuna on top.
4 Season really well with salt and pepper, cover with the top half of the baguette and push down on the whole sandwich really hard to flatten it slightly.
5 Cut the baguette into four pieces and wrap them each up very tightly in clingfilm. Put the 4 sandwiches in the fridge and press them down with a heavy weight. A good cookbook will do the trick.
6 Leave them in the fridge for an hour, then eat and enjoy.

Makes 4 sandwiches

Preparation time 15 minutes (and an hour in the fridge)

1 large, very crusty baguette

1 garlic clove

Olive oil

White wine vinegar

2 large ripe tomatoes, sliced

1 large red onion, halved and thinly sliced

1 sweet red pepper, sliced

2 hard-boiled eggs, sliced

A handful of pitted black olives, cut in half

150g tin tuna

Salt and freshly ground black pepper

Crispy duck pancakes

The highlight for Archie when we eat out at our local Chinese restaurant is the crispy duck pancakes. He loves making them and, as he has got older, the ratio of duck in the pancake, as opposed to on the table or floor, has dramatically increased. Most recipes for crispy duck involve drying out the bird, hanging it and roasting it slowly. It will not surprise you to know that I do not feel this method is in any way appropriate for this book. All the more so because bunging a few duck legs in the oven for an hour actually gets equally crispy and delicious results. What I really love about duck legs is that they are virtually impossible to overcook. Any dish that gives me the leeway to forget I was cooking it and still be more than edible gets my seal of approval.

Preheat your oven to 200°C/400°F/Gas Mark 6.

1 Pat the duck legs dry with some kitchen paper, season them well with salt and pepper and then give them a really good dusting with the five spice powder. Put them in a baking dish and roast for an hour. No need to baste them or anything, just let the skin go naturally crispy.
2 Slice the cucumber into two chunks, 6cm in length. Cut the chunks lengthways into 5mm thick slices and then cut the slices lengthways to give cucumber matchsticks.
3 Chop the top and bottom off the spring onions, cut them in half and slice them finely.
4 When the duck is ready it should be soft and tender and just pull away from the bone. Serve it warm in the middle of the table with the cucumber, the spring onions, the hoi sin sauce and the pancakes.

Serves 4

Preparation time 5 minutes

Cooking time 1 hour

2 large duck legs

Salt and freshly ground black pepper

A really big pinch of Chinese five spice powder

½ cucumber, peeled

4 spring onions

Hoi sin sauce

8 Chinese wheat pancakes (these are sold in most supermarkets)

Chinese lettuce wraps

Another Asian-style lunch bite – and another one for everyone to put together at the table. When we eat as a family, we really enjoy this small element of play and interactivity. Spillages and droppages are part of the fun, especially with a little toddler in the midst. Make this with beef, chicken, pork or vegetarian mince.

1 In a large pan on a medium-high heat, soften the onion, garlic and ginger for 4 to 5 minutes in a glug of vegetable oil or sunflower oil.
2 Add the meat and continue to stir for a few minutes while it cooks and breaks up.
3 Mix in the soy sauce, the hoi sin sauce, the vinegar, the water chestnuts and the spring onions and continue to stir and cook for 3 to 4 minutes. Drizzle in a little sesame oil right at the end, just for flavouring.
4 Arrange the lettuce around the edge of a big plate and put the filling in a big bowl in the middle of the plate.
5 At the table, spoon some filling into the lettuce leaves, roll up and eat immediately.

Serves 4

Preparation time 10 minutes

Cooking time 15 minutes

1 small onion, finely chopped or grated

2 garlic cloves, crushed

1.5cm cube of fresh ginger, grated

Vegetable or sunflower oil, for cooking

350g beef, chicken, pork or vegetarian mince

1 tablespoon soy sauce (light or dark)

3 tablespoons hoi sin sauce

2 teaspoons rice wine vinegar (or white wine vinegar)

225g tin sliced water chestnuts, finely chopped

5 spring onions, finely sliced

Sesame oil, for flavouring

12 large crispy lettuce leaves, such as iceberg

My Dad's Thursday Welsh rarebit

When I was growing up, Thursday evenings were 'bread and cheese' night, partly out of necessary frugality, partly out of practicality. We'd have crispy fresh white bread and strong Cheddar while watching Anneka Rice on *Treasure Hunt* and the basketball on Channel 4. Occasionally we would have a variation on a theme and my dad would proudly make his version of a Welsh rarebit.

Heat up the grill in your oven.

1   Toast the bread. If the slices are too soft, the cheese sauce will make them soggy.
2   In a saucepan on a low heat, melt the cheese with the milk (or ale) and the butter.
3   When the cheese has melted, turn the heat up to medium and mix in the egg.
4   Add the flour and keep stirring swiftly until it has been fully mixed in.
5   Take the sauce off the heat and mix in the Worcester sauce and the mustard.
6   Butter the slices of toast and lay them on a baking sheet.
7   Spoon the cheese sauce on to the toasts, sprinkle some paprika on each slice and grill until the cheese goes golden and starts to bubble. Serve immediately.

Makes 4 slices

Preparation time 10 minutes

Cooking time 10–15 minutes

4 thick slices of fresh, crusty white bread

250g extra-mature Cheddar or any other aged hard cheese, grated

100ml milk or (my preferred choice) light brown ale

25g butter, plus extra for spreading

1 beaten egg

1 tablespoon plain flour

Several dashes of Worcester sauce

1 tablespoon mustard (French if you like it strong, American if you prefer it mild)

Paprika, to sprinkle on the cheese

Savoury Brittany pancakes

My ham and cheese pancakes were incredibly popular in the very early days of the blog. Judging by the comments received, I think a lot of people hadn't really thought of doing savoury pancakes, as opposed to sweet ones. Savoury pancakes are also surprisingly quick to rustle up and make a pleasant change from toasted sandwiches. This version follows the classic Brittany recipe, which uses buckwheat flour, giving the pancakes the distinctive nutty brown colour you find in traditional creperies. If you don't have buckwheat flour, don't worry, you can simply replace the quantity with plain flour.

1 Mix all the pancake ingredients together to get a creamy batter. The batter should be runny but not thin, smooth but not thick. If you have time, leave it to rest for 30 minutes in the fridge, but that really is not obligatory.
2 Heat up the pan on a medium heat and drop in a small dollop of butter (about half a teaspoon). Shake the handle and swirl the butter around the pan.
3 Take hold of the frying pan with one hand and, with the other, pour in a ladle of the pancake batter. Tilt the pan in several directions so that the batter covers the whole base.
4 Cook the pancake quickly until the batter is no longer liquid on the top. Turn the pancake over using a spatula and cook for a further 30 seconds.
5 Turn the pancake back over and immediately spoon the filling of your choice onto the middle of the pancake, so it covers a square of roughly 10 x 10cm.
6 Fold the edges of the pancake, one by one, over the filling as if you are sealing the four flaps of a large box. You may find it helps to quickly mark a square around the filling by gently indenting the tip of the spatula into the pancake.
7 Carry on cooking the pancake for 30 seconds on both sides so the filling can warm up and serve immediately.

The following pancake mix can make up to 10 pancakes. Cooked pancakes freeze perfectly and reheat easily in the pan.

Preparation time 10 minutes

Cooking time 3–4 minutes for each pancake

You will need an 8 inch (20cm) non-stick pan

For the dough:
75g plain flour

75g buckwheat flour

350ml milk

2 eggs

A pinch of salt

1 tablespoon melted butter (or a good drop of vegetable oil)

A large knob of butter, for cooking

For the fillings:

The Classic: Ham and Emmental or Gruyère cheese

The Savoyard: Leftover cooked potatoes, Bayonne ham
(or similar) and raclette cheese

The Italian: Sliced tomato, grated mozzarella and basil leaves

The Oceanic: Smoked salmon, crème fraîche, chives and a
squeeze of lemon

The French: Slices of Brie and crispy bacon

The Leafy: Fresh spinach and grated Cheddar cheese

White bean hummus with a tomato and basil salsa

As I have said many times on my blog, I am not sure we could survive without hummus in our house. It would be no exaggeration to say that there are some weeks when Archie eats it three times for lunch, in its various forms. Store-bought hummus can be very good quality so I saw no point in putting a classic chickpea hummus into this book. This hummus is rather different though, as it is made in an Italian style with cannellini beans. It makes for a slightly smoother – and perhaps lighter – hummus and goes wonderfully well with the tomatoes and basil. As it is a 'blitz together' recipe, it doesn't take much longer than opening a pack of hummus from a shop!

You will also need toasted white pitta bread.

1 Make the tomato and basil salsa. Mix the tomato and basil in a bowl together, drizzle in a good drop of olive oil and season with salt and pepper. Set aside.
2 Put all the white bean hummus ingredients (except the olive oil, salt and pepper) in a food mixer or blender and blitz until you get a smooth paste.
3 Season with salt and pepper to taste, then drizzle in a couple of tablespoons of the olive oil and give the hummus one last blitz in the blender.
4 Divide the hummus on to four plates. With the back of a spoon, make a little well in the middle of each portion and spoon the tomato salsa into it, drizzling the hummus with some of the salsa's oil as you go.
5 Serve with toasted flat breads or pitta.

Serves 4 for lunch

Preparation time 10 minutes

For the tomato and basil salsa:
2 very ripe tomatoes, deseeded and chopped

8 basil leaves, finely chopped

Olive oil

Salt and freshly ground black pepper

For the white bean hummus:
400g tin cannellini beans, drained and rinsed

1 garlic clove

Juice of ½ lemon

2 tablespoons tahini paste

½ teaspoon ground cumin

Extra virgin olive oil

Pinch of salt and freshly ground black pepper

Sloppy joe beef buns

My first ever sloppy joe was in Houston on an unplanned stopover on the way back from our honeymoon. Already exhausted and more than a little fed up with the general incompetence of the airline concerned, Jo and I found ourselves in a classic American diner on a highway not far from our hotel. The sloppy joe was, well, sloppy – minced beef in a delicious tomato sauce, overloaded into an already large bun, served with the some of the best chips I can remember having. This version is easy to make and, if our own house is anything to go by, will be a huge success with kids and parents alike.

1 In a frying pan on a medium heat, pour in a glug of olive oil and brown the beef mince for a couple of minutes.
2 Add the onion and the green pepper and continue to stir for 4 more minutes, breaking up the beef mince as you go.
3 Mix in the garlic powder, the mustard, the ketchup and the sugar and simmer for 20 minutes.
4 Season with salt and pepper and serve in the soft baps.

Makes 4

Preparation time 10 minutes

Cooking time 30 minutes

Olive oil

400g lean beef mince

1 small onion, grated

1 small green pepper, finely chopped

½ teaspoon garlic powder or 1 garlic clove, crushed

1 teaspoon Dijon mustard (or similar)

6 tablespoons ketchup (I like to use the reduced-salt and sugar one)

1½ tablespoons soft brown sugar

Salt and freshly ground black pepper

4 soft white baps

Cooking a great omelette (in less than 5 minutes!)

Soon after the blog was launched, I filmed an omelette time challenge. I put up a stop watch and wanted to see how long it took to prepare an omelette from fridge to plate. It took 3 minutes and 50 seconds and showed just how easy and quick it can be to make a fresh and nutritious dish. There wasn't even any cheating involved and the omelette itself was not a blob of blancmange. Omelettes need to be cooked quickly – and on a high heat – to really work. So here is my basic omelette technique and some filling suggestions.

As the cooking involves such a high heat and quick handling of the pan, Archie's role is reduced to mixing and passing me the ingredients (usually eating them before they hit the pan!)

1 In a bowl, mix the egg(s) and a drizzle of milk. Go lightly and don't whisk or mix them too much.
2 Heat up the pan on a very high heat. Throw in a knob of butter and let it melt and foam, but don't let it burn.
3 As soon as the butter is bubbling, pour in the egg mixture.
4 Stand back, resist all temptation to touch the pan, and count to 5 for a one-egg omelette, 8 for a two-egg omelette and 10 for a three-egg omelette.
5 You will see that the omelette is now virtually cooked. Tilt the pan forwards, pull the far tip of the omelette slightly towards you with a spatula or wooden spoon, and let any remaining mixture flow to the base of the frying pan. Depending on the size of your omelette, you may need to do this once or twice.
6 Your omelette is now ready to have the filling thrown in. If you are using cheese, it will melt in the time it takes to serve the omelette.
7 To serve, tilt the pan 45 degrees to the side, allow the edge of the omelette to slip on to a plate and roll the rest of the omelette over itself by turning the frying pan towards the plate.

You will need a non-stick 7 inch (18cm) pan

For the basic omelette:
I found 1 egg sufficed for Archie when he was very little. He now is happy with a 2-egg omelette (and I often use 3 for me).

A dash of milk

A good knob of butter

For the fillings:

It is important to pour fillings on to the omelette, rather than the omelette on to the fillings. If you have any ingredients that need to be cooked, such as mushrooms, they need to be fried and taken out of the pan before cooking the omelette.

You can jazz up any omelette by adding chopped herbs such as thyme, parsley, chives, tarragon and chervil, alone or combined with the egg mix.

Try:
The Classic: Ham, grated Cheddar cheese and chopped tomato

The Cheesy-Leekie: Thinly slice some leek, fry it in butter andthrow it on to the cooked omelette with thinly sliced Camembert

The Norwegian: A few strips of smoked salmon and a few small dollops of cream cheese

The French: Thinly slice some onion and a few chestnut mushrooms and gently fry them until soft. Add them to the omelette with a few slithers of creamy Brie.

Bready scrolls

These bready scrolls are really ingenious and have become a regular feature when we make lunch. Archie loves making them with me – and loves eating them even more. The dough is rustled up in a matter of seconds, is easy to roll out, fun to fill, quick to roll up and bakes in minutes. I could actually write a whole chapter just on fillings, but once you have made this dough once, you will quite likely keep coming back to the recipe and just filling it with whatever you have to hand.

Here's how to make the basic dough, together with five options for fillings.

Preheat your oven to 180ºC/350ºF/Gas Mark 4.

1 In a bowl, using your fingertips, crumble the butter into the flour.
2 Make a well in the middle, pour in the milk and mix to form a soft dough.
3 Knead the dough on a lightly floured surface until all the ingredients are well mixed. Keep the kneading quick and light.
4 Roll the dough out into a rectangle, approximately 30 x 25cm.
5 Spread the filling of your choice over the dough, then roll it up tightly like a Swiss roll (starting from a long edge).
6 Use a sharp knife to cut the roll into scrolls about 3cm wide.
7 Brush the scrolls with a little milk and bake them on non-stick baking trays (or trays lined with non-stick paper) for around 15 minutes, until they have gone golden.

For the fillings:

Green pesto, freshly grated Parmesan and Parma ham

Tomato purée (preferably sun-dried, but classic tomato purée will work too), Parmesan and basil leaves

Ham and Emmental cheese

And finally...my favourite (and it works even better at breakfast time): strong Cheddar and Marmite. You'll either love it or you'll hate it!

Makes about 10

Preparation time
10–15 minutes

Cooking time 15 minutes

For the dough:
40g butter, soft and at room temperature

300g self-raising flour

180ml milk (semi-skimmed is fine), plus extra for glazing the dough

Salmon and cream cheese filo parcels

I wanted to make a salmon en croûte for this book, but was keen to find a little playful twist, hence the use of filo pastry instead of puff pastry. As with the feta and cream cheese tart (see page 40), filo pastry is a lot of fun for kids to handle and wrapping these little parcels is a lovely bit of creative play in the kitchen. When I used to live in France, I loved the herby cream cheeses available there and I use a home-made version in these salmon parcels, which adds loads of flavour and helps keep the salmon nice and moist. This recipe makes four small-sized parcels for a midday snack, but can easily be doubled for an evening meal or bigger lunch.

Preheat your oven to 200°C/400°F/Gas Mark 6.

1 In a bowl, mix together the cream cheese, dill, basil, lemon zest and season well with some salt and pepper.
2 Melt the butter in a non-metallic bowl in the microwave for 30-40 seconds (or in a pan on the hob).
3 You need to work pretty quickly with the filo sheets so they don't dry out (cover them with a slightly damp cloth while you are preparing all the parcels). Cut the sheets and the salmon fillets in half, widthways. Take one sheet and brush it with the melted butter. Put another sheet on top of it, brush with butter again and place a final sheet on top, brushing again with butter.
4 Place one piece of salmon on the prepared buttered filo sheets and then put a quarter of the cream cheese mix on top.
5 Now you need to wrap the salmon. Bring the filo pastry sheets up over the salmon and scrunch them together to close the parcel. Repeat the process for the other three parcels.
6 Brush a baking sheet with some melted butter, put the parcels on it and brush them with the last of the butter.
7 Bake the parcels for around 20 minutes, until they are nice and crisp. Serve them with a green salad. Although they are best when warm, they are also surprisingly good when cooled down.

Serves 4 as a snack

Preparation time 15 minutes

Cooking time 20–25 minutes

100g cream cheese

A handful of dill, chopped

A handful of basil leaves, finely chopped

Zest of 1 lemon, grated

Salt and freshly ground black pepper

5 tablespoons butter

6 sheets of filo pastry (available in all supermarkets)

2 x 175g thick salmon fillets, skin and grey flesh removed

Green salad, leaves to serve

Cheat's cheese and onion tart

I love making tarts, but sometimes it can be a long, stop-start, multi-stage process – and hence not always ideal for cooking with little helpers around. This is somewhat a cheat's tart. I mean, it doesn't even use a tin! Once the onions are cooked, the tart is very easily assembled, with the humble onions becoming something really rather tasty indeed.

Preheat the oven to 180°C/350°F/Gas Mark 4.

1 Heat up a large frying pan, pour in a large glug of olive oil and stir in the onion. Put a lid on the pan and leave the onion to cook on a gentle heat for 10 to 12 minutes. Keep an eye on it and stir occasionally so that it doesn't burn.

2 Turn the heat up, stir in the sugar and the white wine vinegar and continue to cook, uncovered, for a further 4 to 5 minutes. The onion should be now be soft and golden.

3 Season the onion with salt and pepper.

4 Unroll the pastry on to a lightly floured baking tray. You want a square or circle (depending on which brand of pastry you found) that is approximately 30cm wide.

5 Prick the pastry liberally with a fork then sprinkle most of the cheese on to the base, leaving a border of 5cm.

6 Spread the cooked onion on to the cheese.

7 Fold the edges of the pastry back to the edges of the onion to create a 2cm border. Brush the rim with the milk or egg and sprinkle the rest of the cheese over the pastry borders.

8 Bake for approximately 25 minutes until the pastry has puffed up and is golden. Serve immediately with a green salad.

Serves 4

Preparation time 5–10 minutes

Cooking time 45 minutes

Olive oil

4 large onions, cut in half and thinly sliced

2 tablespoons soft brown sugar

2–3 tablespoons white wine vinegar

Salt and freshly ground black pepper

1 pack of pre-rolled puff pastry

175g grated cheese (Emmental or Gruyère work best and Cheddar works too)

Some milk or a beaten egg, to brush the pastry

Lamb kofta pittas with a pomegranate salad

It was one of our earliest surprises that Archie loves pomegranate seeds. They were a magical way of keeping him quiet too as he studiously tried to remove the inner part of the seed. Of course we knew it was impossible, but we were hardly going to spoil his fun, were we?! These kofta pittas make for a great lunch, but you can easily serve them for supper by upping the quantities. I use a pack of fresh pomegranate seeds, but it can be a lot of fun allowing your kids to deseed a fresh pomegranate, although it will test your mess threshold to its absolute limit! Remember – pomegranate stains, very permanently.

1 In a bowl, mix together the lamb mince, the ground cumin, coriander and cinnamon, the fresh mint and fresh coriander, a pinch of salt and some ground pepper. Divide the mixture into four and roll each portion into a sausage shape.
2 Pour a light drizzle of olive oil into a frying pan on a medium heat and cook the koftas for 7 to 8 minutes, rolling them from time to time, until they are browned and cooked through. When they are cooked, take them out of the pan and set aside on a plate.
3 Warm the pittas either in a toaster or under the grill.
4 Serve the koftas with the yoghurt, the extra mint, the lemon, the pomegranate seeds and all the salad stuff at the table and let everyone assemble their own lunch in the warm pittas.

Serves 4

Preparation time 15 minutes

Cooking time 10 minutes

400g lamb mince

1 teaspoon ground cumin

1 teaspoon ground coriander

A pinch of ground cinnamon

20g mint leaves, half chopped, the other half saved for serving

10g coriander leaves, chopped

Salt and freshly ground black pepper

Olive oil

To serve:
4 pitta breads

150ml Greek yoghurt

1 lemon, for squeezing

1 pack of fresh pomegranate seeds

½ small cucumber, chopped

2 lovely ripe tomatoes, chopped

2 good handfuls of shredded lettuce

Leftover chicken fried rice

This is a perfect quick weekday lunch, especially if you have made a chicken roast recently and have leftover meat. It's a version of the street-food rice you find in the Far East, where speed and ease of preparation are key, making it perfect for this book. I always somehow manage to cook too much rice and this is a welcome way of using it up. If you don't have any leftover rice, you can use a ready-to-cook pack too, but don't use freshly cooked rice because it will go all sticky when you stir the egg into it.

1 Heat a wok (or frying pan) on a medium heat. Tip in the garlic, stir for a few seconds, then add the onion and fry for a couple of minutes.
2 Pour in the two eggs, let them set a little, and then continue to stir so they scramble and mix in with the onion and garlic.
3 Add in the shredded chicken, followed by the sugar, the curry powder and a squirt of tomato purée. Mix it all together well.
4 Add the peas and half a small glass of water and leave to cook for 3 minutes, stirring as you go.
5 Mix in the cooked rice and a few good dashes of soy sauce. Make sure everything is piping hot and then serve immediately.

Serves 4

Preparation time 5 minutes

Cooking time 10 minutes

2 garlic cloves, finely chopped

1 onion, finely chopped or grated

2 eggs, beaten

Leftover chicken (maybe about 200g), cut into shreds

1 teaspoon caster sugar

½ tablespoon curry powder (or more if you prefer a stronger flavour)

A squirt of tomato purée

A good handful of frozen peas

450g leftover cooked rice (approx)

Soy sauce

Vegetable oil

Baked aubergines (imam bayildi)

I love this dish, as much as anything for the story behind the name. Imam bayildi means 'the Imam swooned (or fainted)' when he first ate this. Don't worry, it doesn't contain noxious substances. I am presuming he fainted simply because of the wonderful mix of flavours and the delicious melting aubergine scooped onto warm flatbreads, finished off with some thick yoghurt. As is often the case with traditional dishes such as this, there are more versions than days in a lifetime. Here's mine to add to the already long list.

Preheat your oven to 180°C/350°F/Gas Mark 4.

1 Cut the aubergine in half lengthways and gouge out the flesh with a spoon (it comes away really easily), leaving a 'wall' of about 5mm. Coarsely chop up the aubergine flesh you have removed.

2 In a pan on a medium heat, pour in about one third of the olive oil and gently fry the onion for 5 minutes, until it starts to soften.

3 Add the garlic and stir for a minute, then add the aubergine and the cumin and continue to cook for a few more minutes. The aubergine will absorb much of the oil.

4 Throw in the tomatoes and the herbs and continue to cook for 3 to 4 more minutes. Season with salt and pepper.

5 Put the aubergine skins in a baking dish and fill them with the cooked mixture. Sprinkle them with the sugar, drizzle over the lemon juice and gently pour over the rest of the olive oil.

6 Bake the aubergine halves for 35 to 40 minutes, until they are really tender. You can baste them with some of the oil in the baking dish halfway through if you want. By the time they are cooked, they will be 'swimming' in a fair amount of very flavoursome olive oil. Spoon some of it back over the baked aubergines.

7 You can serve the imam bayildi immediately, but leaving it to cool for an hour at room temperature will significantly improve it. Serve with lots of thick yoghurt and warm pittas or flatbreads.

Serves 4 for lunch

Preparation time 15 minutes (plus an hour cooling if possible)

Cooking time 50–55 minutes

1 large aubergine

150ml olive oil

1 onion, finely chopped or grated

3 garlic cloves, crushed

1½ teaspoons ground cumin

200g tin chopped tomatoes

1 small bunch of basil, leaves roughly chopped

1 small bunch of flat-leaf parsley, chopped

Salt and freshly ground black pepper

1½ teaspoons sugar

Juice of ½ lemon

Thick yoghurt and warm pitta bread or flatbreads, to serve

Savoury muffins

I would never have thought that a humble muffin could be so popular. When I asked readers of my blog what existing recipes, if any, they would like to see in the book, the muffins were the unanimous favourite. This recipe has consistently been one of the most visited of the whole site and many people have told me that they now regularly bake savoury muffins. The base mix of egg, flour, oil and milk can be complemented by any combination of cheeses, cold meats and vegetables that you happen to have to hand, to make muffins that can be eaten at breakfast, snack time or lunch. Vegetables such as carrots and courgettes don't even need to be precooked. They can simply be grated and added to the mix. This really is the ultimate flexible recipe. And because it involves so much cold mixing, it's a great recipe to introduce kids into the kitchen with too. Mind you, I am not for a moment saying that these are solely a kids' snack. Many a parent has reported to me about making these muffins with their children before their morning nap and there not being many left for lunch by the time their children woke up!

Muffin tins vary in size, but this mix will make 9–12 large muffins in one or two muffin tins.

Preheat your oven to 200°C/400°F/Gas Mark 6.

1 Cook the broccoli florets in shallow boiling water until they are soft. Drain, cool them down with cold water and chop them coarsely.
2 Mix together the cheese and the flour, then mix in the broccoli and tomatoes.
3 Add the milk, olive oil and egg and mix to a lumpy, fairly thick batter. Season to taste with salt and pepper.
4 Lightly oil the muffin tins and fill each individual cup to the top with the muffin mix.
5 Bake in the middle of the oven for 20 minutes. The muffins are ready when they are golden on top and fairly dense to the touch. Best served warm, 5 to 10 minutes after coming out of the oven.

Makes 9–12 large muffins

Preparation time 15 minutes

Cooking time 30 minutes

4 large broccoli florets

100g grated extra-mature Cheddar cheese

225g self-raising flour

12 cherry tomatoes, deseeded and chopped

175ml milk

55ml olive oil

1 egg

Salt and freshly ground black pepper

2 | Lighter Bites

63

3
Super Bowls

These recipes are more than soups. They are filling meals in their own right. They are a brilliant – and nearly always economical – way of serving warming and hearty meals for a whole family, especially in the colder autumn and winter months.

Chorizo and chickpea soup

This delicious, soul-warming dish is right on the cusp of a
soup and a stew and is definitely a meal in a bowl. In fact, the
only thing that turns it into a soup is the chicken stock. If you
would prefer to enjoy this more as a classic stew, just add in
200ml chicken stock instead of the litre required for the soup.
Still, I much prefer it as a soup and we serve it with lots of
crispy fresh bread and butter to mop up all the lovely juices.

1 Heat a good glug of the olive oil in the pan on a medium
   heat and cook the chorizo for a minute or two.
2 Stir in the onion, carrot, celery, garlic and cumin, turn the
   heat down and put the lid on the pan.
3 Leave the vegetables and chorizo to slowly cook for 8 to 10
   minutes in the covered pan.
4 Pour in the tomatoes, the stock, the chickpeas and the
   cabbage or kale, season with a little salt and pepper, bring
   to the boil then leave to simmer gently for 25 to 30 minutes.
5 Turn off the heat, mix in the parsley, season again if
   necessary and leave the soup for a further 2 minutes
   before serving.

Serves 4

Preparation time 10 minutes

Cooking time 40–45 minutes

You will need a deep pan
with a lid

Olive oil

150g good-quality chorizo
sausage, chopped into
small pieces

1 onion, roughly chopped

1 carrot, roughly chopped

1 stick of celery, roughly
chopped

1 garlic clove, crushed

1 teaspoon ground cumin
(optional)

400g tin good-quality
chopped tomatoes

1 litre chicken stock

400g tin chickpeas

250g Savoy cabbage or kale,
coarsely chopped

Salt and freshly ground
black pepper

A handful of chopped flat-leaf
parsley, to serve

Pasta and bean soup

Similar in cooking style to the chickpea and chorizo soup on the previous page, this Italian take on a meal-in-a-soup has a very different flavour and texture. This recipe is loosely based on a *ribollita*, which literally means 're-boiled', because the Italians would always say that it is better the day after it is cooked. Personally, I think this soup tastes great whenever you eat it. If you are vegetarian, you can happily leave out the bacon. The soup will lose a little of its flavour, but will still be deliciously satisfying, especially if you use a good quality olive oil and a strong Parmesan.

1 Bring your chicken stock to the boil before cooking the soup.
2 Add 1 tablespoon olive oil to a large saucepan and fry the bacon on a medium heat until it starts to go crispy. Take the bacon out of the saucepan and drain on a paper towel.
3 Add a few more glugs of olive oil and cook the onion, garlic, celery and carrot for 3 to 4 minutes so that they soften up a little but do not brown.
4 Mix the bacon back in, add the chicken stock, squirt in the tomato purée, bring to the boil then turn the heat down and leave to simmer for 5 minutes.
5 Crush approximately half of the beans with a fork. Pour in the crushed and whole beans and the pasta and cook for a further 10 to 12 minutes, until the pasta is cooked.
6 Mix in the parsley and season with salt and pepper to taste. Serve with a little olive oil drizzled over the top and lashings of Parmesan cheese.

Serves 4

Preparation time 10 minutes

Cooking time 30 minutes

1 litre good-quality chicken stock

Olive oil (the more flavoursome the better)

100g cured or smoked bacon (not too fatty), chopped into small pieces

1 onion, finely chopped or grated

1 garlic clove, chopped

2 sticks of celery, finely chopped or grated

2 carrots, finely chopped or grated

2 good squirts of tomato purée (or 2 tablespoons)

500g tinned borlotti or haricot beans, drained

150g small macaroni

2 tablespoons chopped flat-leaf parsley

Salt and freshly ground black paper

Freshly grated Parmesan cheese, to serve

Moroccan harira soup

I was lucky throughout my twenties to live in the city of
Lille in Northern France. It was vibrant, cultural and very
cosmopolitan, thanks mainly to its wonderful North African
community. On a Sunday morning, the huge main square of
the suburb of Wazemmes was turned into a bustling ethnic
market, the highlight of which for me were all the food sellers.
It was there that I discovered harira. Traditionally served at
the end of the Ramadan fast, harira is the original meal in one
bowl. Although it requires a relatively long cooking time, it
is very quick to put together and involves no cooking of the
ingredients prior to simmering it – you just throw everything
in the pan. It goes without saying that it is a perfect freezing
soup too and we have cooked this with double or even triple
quantities to make it last several meals.

As always with my dishes, you can be pretty approximate
with the quantities of spices – a little more or less of
something is not going to ruin such a robust dish. Neither will
missing out an ingredient or two. You can also omit the lamb
if you wish. The flavour will be slightly less rich, but the soup
will be no less tasty for it.

1 Take a large saucepan and throw in the lamb, the lentils,
   the onion, the spices, salt and pepper, the tomatoes, the
   chicken stock and 1 litre water.
2 Bring to the boil, then skim off the froth from the surface,
   put the lid on, turn down the heat and leave to simmer for
   between 1½ and 2 hours.
3 Add the chickpeas and rice and cook for a further 30
   minutes.
4 Right at the end, stir in the fresh coriander and the lemon
   juice.
5 Serve with lemon wedges and fresh warm flatbreads.

Serves 6–8

Preparation time 15 minutes

Cooking time 2–2½ hours

750g diced lamb (any cut
will do)

100g Puy lentils

1 onion, finely chopped

½ teaspoon ground
cinammon

½ teaspoon turmeric

½ teaspoon ground coriander

½ teaspoon ground cumin

A pinch of ground ginger

A pinch of paprika

Salt and freshly ground
black pepper

400g tin tomatoes

1 litre chicken stock

240g tin chickpeas, drained

100g long-grain rice

A handful of coriander,
finely chopped

A good squeeze of
lemon juice

Lemon wedges and
flatbreads, to seeve

Easy ramen noodle soup (chicken, salmon, tofu)

When I moved back from living in France for ten years in 2000, one of the first 'novelties' I discovered (well, a novelty for me at least) was Japanese food, and more specifically noodle soups in large canteen-style restaurants. I loved the simple flavours of the soups and the obligatory slurping suited me well. It is hard to imagine a more complete balanced meal in a bowl – or an easier one to prepare. This noodle soup is very flexible – you get three versions here, all equally satisfying – and you can easily substitute ingredients in and out of the recipe and the dish will still work brilliantly.

1 Cook the noodles according to the instructions on the packet, then drain and cool them under cold water and drizzle some oil through them so they don't stick together.
2 Bring your stock to the boil.
3 At the same time, heat up a wok or deep frying pan. Add a good drizzle of vegetable oil and cook the garlic, ginger and lemon grass for no more than a minute. Make sure you stir vigorously or else the garlic will burn.
4 Add in the chicken, salmon or tofu and cook for 3 to 4 minutes. If you are cooking the salmon, stir gently or else the cubes will disintegrate.
5 Throw on a good dash of the soy sauce and take the wok off the heat.
6 Pile a handful of noodles at the bottom of four large deep bowls.
7 Share out the wok mix equally on top of each pile of noodles, sprinkle the carrot and mange tout over the mix and then pour in enough boiling stock to barely cover the pile. The stock will cook the carrot and mange tout in the few minutes it will take to serve the bowls.
8 You can drizzle over extra soy sauce if you want the soup to be saltier or drizzle in some chilli oil to give it a little kick.

Serves 4

Preparation time 10 minutes

Cooking time 10–15 minutes

For the base soup:
250g ramen noodles (you can also use soba or udon noodles or, indeed, classic Chinese noodles)

1.5 litres good-quality chicken (or vegetable) stock

A little vegetable oil

1 garlic clove, chopped

2.5cm cube of fresh ginger, grated

1 stalk of lemon grass, chopped

Soy sauce (preferably Japanese)

For chicken:
2 large chicken fillets, cut into thin strips

For salmon:
3 x 150g salmon fillets, skin and grey flesh removed and cut into cubes

For tofu:
250g tofu, cut into cubes

To garnish:
2 carrots, grated

150g mange tout (or sugar snap peas), very finely sliced

Cabbage, lentil and bacon soup

This is a lovely, chunky, hearty and warming soup, packed with vegetables and a true meal in its own right when served with big chunks of fresh crusty bread and butter. No need to be too precise in your chopping here – this is a rustic soup without pretence. If you prefer a vegetarian version, simply omit the bacon and use vegetable instead of chicken stock.

1 In a large saucepan on a medium heat, pour in a good glug of olive oil and fry the bacon for a minute or so, then add the onion, leek, celery and carrot and cook for 5 minutes, until the vegetables start to soften.
2 Pour in the stock, squirt in a bit of tomato purée, bring the soup to the boil and simmer for 15 minutes.
3 Stir in the cabbage and lentils and cook for a further 5–6 minutes.
4 Season with salt and pepper, stir in the chopped parsley and serve with crusty bread and some freshly grated Parmesan.

Serves 4

Preparation time 10 minutes

Cooking time 25 minutes

Olive oil

6 rashers of pancetta or streaky bacon, chopped

1 onion, chopped

1 leek, trimmed, cut in half lengthways and sliced

2 sticks of celery, chopped

2 carrots, chopped

1 litre good-quality vegetable or chicken stock

A couple of squirts of tomato purée

300g Savoy cabbage, finely sliced

400g tin lentils, rinsed and drained

Salt and freshly ground black pepper

A small handful of flat-leaf parsley, chopped

Crusty bread and freshly grated Parmesan cheese, to serve

Manhattan crab chowder

A Manhattan chowder is a tomato-based soup, unlike its more famous, creamy New England cousin. Indeed, legend has it that there is actually a law on the New England statute books that a chowder cannot be called a chowder in that state if it has tomatoes in it! Whether you want to call this soup a chowder, or even just a minestrone soup enhanced with tinned crab, it is a lovely winter warmer. Packed with vegetables, it is an extremely filling, delicately flavoured meal in a bowl.

1 Pour a big glug of olive oil into a large saucepan on a medium heat, throw in the onions and gently fry them for 5 minutes until they start to soften.
2 Add the celery, the carrot, the garlic and the courgette and continue to cook for 3-4 minutes, stirring often.
3 Throw in the potatoes and the dried herbs and stir for a further minute or two.
4 Pour in the chicken stock and the chopped tomatoes. Bring to the boil then turn the heat down and simmer the soup for 20 minutes.
5 Mix in the white crab meat and continue to simmer the soup for 10 minutes, or until the potatoes and all the vegetables and soft and cooked.
6 Season with salt and pepper then give the chowder a good stir. Don't be afraid to crush some of the potatoes and other vegetables as this will enhance the texture of the soup.
7 Serve immediately with fresh crusty bread.

Serves 4

Preparation time 15 minutes

Cooking time

Olive oil

1 onion, chopped

3 sticks of celery, chopped

1 carrot, cut into small cubes

3 cloves garlic, chopped

1 large courgette, cut into small cubes

2 potatoes, peeled and cut into small cubes

2 tsp Italian dried herb mix (or any combination of dried basil, oregano and thyme)

2 x small (approximately 150g) tins white crab meat, drained

900ml chicken stock

440g tin chopped tomatoes

Salt and freshly ground black pepper

4

My Daddy Cooks the Classics

You will most probably have eaten these classic dishes before but they get the full 'My Daddy Cooks' treatment in this chapter. These recipes are mainly simplified versions, many with their own original twists, and all with plenty of scope for lots of help from any willing little helpers in the kitchen.

Creamy pork stroganoff

Stroganoff – a word that, no matter how we spin it, Archie just cannot pronounce! Still, Count Stroganoff's nineteenth century contribution to family meals (although I suspect his family lived in rather different surrounds to mine) is a big favourite in our house, not least because it takes less than 20 minutes to cook from start to finish. Because the pork is cooked so quickly, you will want to make sure you use a tenderloin cut or else the meat will be too tough. Traditionally served on rice, this stroganoff is also tasty served with tagliatelle tossed in a little butter.

Depending on what you are serving the stroganoff with, cook some rice or pasta according to the instructions on the packet.

1 Meanwhile, dust the pork with the smoked paprika.
2 In a frying pan, heat the oil over a medium heat and fry the onion for about 4 minutes to soften up.
3 Turn the heat up slightly and add the pork, stirring continuously while cooking for 2 minutes.
4 Add in the mushrooms and cook for a further 2 minutes.
5 Stir in the crème fraîche, bring to the boil, then turn down the heat and bring to a very gentle simmer, throw in the parsley and finally squeeze in the lemon and season.
6 Sprinkle a little extra paprika over and serve immediately.

Serves 4

Preparation time 5–10 minutes

Cooking time 15 minutes

Plain rice or tagliatelle, to serve

500g pork tenderloin, trimmed of fat and cut into thin strips

2 teaspoons smoked paprika (or plain paprika for a milder flavour)

Olive oil

1 large onion, halved and very thinly sliced

200g chestnut mushrooms, halved and thinly sliced

200ml crème fraîche

A good handful of flat-leaf parsley leaves, chopped

A squeeze of lemon juice

Salt and freshly ground black pepper

The My Daddy Cooks spaghetti Bolognese

Of course, spaghetti Bolognese should be slowly and lovingly cooked so that all the flavours have a chance to infuse. But what if you barely have 20 minutes to make supper? Is there a way of getting a great spag bol on to the table? Well, this version may shock the purists – but I would challenge them to guess that this is a speedy version when you serve it to them. The trick lies in grating the vegetables finely. This not only saves a huge amount of time in the preparation, it also means you don't have to cook them for the usual 15 minutes before cooking the rest of the sauce.

1 Put a large saucepan of salted water on to boil and cook your pasta according to the instructions on the packet. Drain and cool it down under cold water when it is ready.

2 Meanwhile, heat up a deep frying pan or wok on a high heat and pour in the olive oil. When the oil is hot, add the onion, celery, carrot and garlic and cook for 3 to 4 minutes, stirring vigorously.

3 Make a little space in the middle of the pan and add the beef. Continue to stir vigorously for 2 to 3 minutes on a high heat until most of the meat is no longer red.

4 Pour in the glass of red wine and allow much of it to be absorbed or evaporate. This should take no more than a couple of minutes.

5 Once only a little bit of the wine remains visible, turn the heat down to medium, pour in the tomato passata and continue to cook on a medium heat for 5 to 6 minutes, stirring regularly.

6 The sauce should by now have thickened. Throw in a really good dash of the Worcester sauce, add the basil and season well with salt and black pepper.

7 Stir in the cooked spaghetti, making sure it all gets well covered with sauce.

8 Leave the pan to rest for a few minutes before serving with loads of Parmesan.

Serves 4

Preparation time 10 minutes

Cooking time 15–20 minutes

450g dried spaghetti

Olive oil

1 onion, finely grated

2 sticks of celery, finely chopped

1 carrot, finely grated

3 garlic cloves, crushed

500g lean beef mince

1 glass of red wine

500ml tomato passata (or a 400g tin chopped tomatoes)

A good dash of Worcester sauce

30g basil, leaves chopped or torn (don't use the stems)

Salt and freshly ground black pepper

Freshly grated Parmesan cheese, to serve

The quickest home-made pizza ever!

We love making pizza in our kitchen. And we love making the dough, letting it rise, knocking it back, making a lovely tomato sauce and cooking it on a hot granite stone in the oven. Except when we have no time. Which is very often. And when we have no time, we love making pizzas this way. These are not pizzas for the purists, but for lunch in a hurry they are absolutely brilliant and a constant hit in our house. As the key here is speed, I cheat on the tomato sauce and none of the other ingredients need to be precooked. Once you have the base mastered, you really can use whatever two or three toppings you have in your kitchen.

Preheat your oven to 220°C/425°F/Gas Mark 7.

1 Make the dough according to the instructions for the bready scrolls and cut it into four portions.
2 Generously flour a large baking tray and pat each of the dough portions out into a fairly thick circle.
3 Squirt some tomato purée or spoon a little passata on each pizza base and spread it thinly. Sprinkle a pinch of oregano on to each one.
4 Scatter 2 or 3 different ingredients on to each pizza, taking care not to overload the base.
5 Sprinkle liberally with the grated cheese and bake for about 10 minutes, or until the cheese has fully melted and the pizza has crisped up.

Makes 4 lunch pizzas

Preparation time 5–10 minutes

Cooking time 10 minutes

1 portion of the dough mix from the bready scrolls on page 54

Tomato purée or tomato passata

A sprinkling of oregano

Any combination of 2 or 3 vegetables or other ingredients you can find in the fridge, freezer or store cupboard (ham, bacon, leftover chicken, tuna, mushrooms, sweetcorn, thinly sliced red onion, thinly sliced asparagus, olives and halved cherry tomatoes, just for starters)

4 handfuls of grated cheese, preferably mozzarella, but Cheddar works too (we are going for practicality here, not authenticity!)

The My Daddy Cooks burger and chips

There are two key tricks that make this burger so succulent and moist. First of all, if you want a really melting burger, there is no point in buying lean mince. The fat in mince actually contributes to a burger's moistness. Go for a beef mince with 20 per cent fat in it. Secondly, I slightly cook the onion before mixing it in with the beef and this extra softness really contributes to both the flavour and texture of the burgers. Add in a dash of Worcester sauce and some fresh thyme and you have got yourself one very delicious burger indeed.

Preheat your oven to near its hottest setting, around 230ºC/450ºF/Gas Mark 8.

1 First make the chips. Cut the potatoes into long wedges by cutting them in half lengthways, then in half again lengthways, and then in half again lengthways.
2 Pat the potatoes dry with some kitchen paper, give them a good drenching in a large bowl with the olive oil and mix in the salt.
3 Lay the potatoes out flat on a baking tray and bake for 25 minutes or until they have gone golden and crispy.
4 When the potatoes go into the oven, heat up a good splash of olive oil in a frying pan on a high heat, add in the grated onion and fry for barely a few minutes. Pour the onion into a bowl so it can quickly cool down.
5 When the onion has all but cooled down after a couple of minutes, mix it with the beef, the Worcester sauce, the thyme, a large pinch of salt and the ground black pepper.
6 Cut the beef mixture into four equal portions, compact each portion in your hands and flatten it out to make a round and moderately thick burger.
7 Meanwhile, with 10 minutes left for the potatoes to cook, heat up a frying pan on a high heat. Brush the burgers with olive oil and cook them for 4 to 5 minutes on both sides, or until cooked through.
8 Toast the buns and serve the burgers with everything – the potatoes, buns, the salad stuff, ketchup, mustard and anything else you fancy – in the middle of your dining table and let everyone build their own burger.

Serves 4

Preparation time 10 minutes

Cooking time 35 minutes

For the oven chips:
2 large baking potatoes

Olive oil

A good pinch of salt

For the burgers:
Olive oil

1 onion, grated

500g beef mince with 20% fat

A dash of Worcester sauce

A few sprigs of thyme (dried thyme can also work)

Salt and freshly ground black pepper

To serve:
4 burger rolls, ciabatta rolls or white baps

Chopped lettuce, a sliced beef tomato and sliced red onion

Home-made fish and chips

Fish and chips is a big favourite in our house. We are fortunate to have a great chippy very nearby and we get fish and chips probably once a month. I always feel like I am slightly shortening my life expectancy, however, when I eat it so it is good to be able to turn to a less fatty home-made version. At home, we bread our fish (this is a brilliantly messy and fun activity for little helpers) and oven cook our chips.

Preheat your oven to 230ºC/450ºF/Gas Mark 8.

1   First make the chips. Peel the potatoes, then take a thin slice off the sides and ends to form a rough rectangular shape. Slice each potato lengthways into 1cm wide slices and then cut each of those slices lengthways into 1cm strips. Pat all the chips dry with kitchen paper, put the chips in a bowl and drizzle with oil, making sure they all get a good coating.
2   Place all the chips in a baking tray in neat rows (and not touching each other) and bake for 35 minutes in the centre of the oven.
3   To prepare the fish, take three wide bowls or plates. In one, mix a good pinch of salt and pepper with the plain flour. In another, gently whisk the egg and in the last one, pour in the breadcrumbs.
4   Dip each fillet of fish first in the flour, covering well and shaking off any excess, then roll in the egg, again covering well, and finally coat in the breadcrumbs, pressing down slightly so the breadcrumbs set nicely.
5   With 10 minutes to go for the chips, heat a large frying pan on a medium heat, add in 3 or 4 tablespoons of oil and cook the fish for 5 to 6 minutes on each side, or until golden and crispy.

Serves 4

Preparation time 15 minutes

Cooking time 45 minutes

2 large floury potatoes

A glug of oil for the chips, plus extra to cook the fish (canola works particularly well for the potatoes, as does rapeseed. Try not to use olive oil if you can.)

Salt and freshly ground black pepper

2–3 tablespoons plain flour

1 egg

150g fine breadcrumbs or matzo meal (you can of course make your own by whizzing some stale bread in a food mixer)

4 thin white fish fillets, 150–170g each

My BBQ ribs

There are few things more satisfying than eating sticky ribs! It's no surprise, therefore, that one of the most popular recipes on the My Daddy Cooks blog has been my slow-cooked sticky pork spareribs. These ribs are very different, but equally moreish, using a marinade that I loosely call a BBQ marinade. In reality, it is just a throw together of all of the sauces and condiments I have in my cupboards! I don't know how or why it works, it just does – and it goes without saying that it is slightly different each time. The ribs can be grilled, barbecued or baked and will definitely benefit from being left to marinate in the fridge, although this is by no means obligatory if you are short of time.

1 Mix all the marinade ingredients together and rub it all over the ribs. Archie loves doing this – the messier the better – I am convinced it helps the flavour. If you don't have 2 or 3 hours to leave the ribs to marinate in the fridge, leave them for at least 5 to 10 minutes in the bowl before you cook them.
2 Cook on a barbecue or under a grill for 20 minutes in total, turning the ribs over halfway through and brushing them with the marinade every 5 minutes or so.
3 If you are using an oven, preheat it to 180°C/350°F/Gas Mark 4 and cook the ribs for an hour or so, turning them in their juices from time to time (you will probably need to add a little water to the pan towards the end of the cooking time). They are ready when they are nice and sticky and golden.
4 Serve with plain rice and a simple salad.

Serves 4

Preparation time 5 minutes

Cooking time 20 minutes on the barbecue or under the grill or 1 hour in the oven

For the marinade:
1 teaspoon sesame oil

2 tablespoons dark soy sauce

A few drops of Thai fish sauce

6 tablespoons honey

1 tablespoon tomato ketchup or tomato purée

A dash of Worcester sauce

1 teaspoon balsamic vinegar

Salt and freshly ground black pepper

1.5kg pork ribs

No-fry Singapore noodles

Here's a change from wok frying this classic curry-flavoured noodle dish, ideal if you have the very youngest little helpers in the kitchen with you. I cook all the ingredients in a baking dish in the oven – and then all that remains is to mix in the cooked noodles. This method won't win you many (any?) awards for authenticity, but the very tasty resulting dish won't be met with any complaints from a hungry family.

Preheat your oven to 220°C/425°F/Gas Mark 7.

1 Throw the onion, garlic, ginger, carrot, courgette and red pepper into a baking dish, mix in a good glug of oil and bake in the oven for 20 minutes.
2 Add the chicken, the prawns, several dashes of the soy sauce, the curry powder and the turmeric to the baking dish and mix it all together well. Bake in the oven for a further 10 minutes (stirring once or twice), or until the prawns and chicken are cooked through.
3 Cook the noodles as per the instructions on the packet. Try to time them to be ready at the end of the cooking time for the dish in the oven. Drain them in a colander.
4 When the chicken and prawns are cooked, take the dish out of the oven and add a pinch of salt and some ground pepper.
5 Stir the noodles into the baking dish, coating them well with all the flavours and ingredients.
6 Serve immediately with lime wedges.

Serves 4

Preparation time 10 minutes

Cooking time 30 minutes

1 onion, thinly sliced

1 garlic clove, crushed

A small cube of fresh ginger, grated

1 carrot, grated

1 courgette, grated

1 red pepper, deseeded and thinly sliced

Groundnut oil (or similar flavourless oil)

1 chicken breast, diced

100g frozen peeled raw king prawns, defrosted

Soy sauce

2–3 teaspoons curry powder

A good pinch of turmeric

250g rice noodles

Salt and freshly ground black pepper

Lime wedges, to serve

Mexican lasagne

Take an easy chilli con carne, layer it into a 'lasagne' using plain flour tortillas, top it with cheese and crème fraîche and the result is possibly my favourite dish in the whole book. The big surprise is how moist the tortillas go, absorbing the delicious juices from the chilli. Archie loves layering the dish (or 'building the house', as he calls it) and with the added advantage of being a fully make-ahead recipe, this twist on two classic dishes is a big winner every time.

Preheat your oven to 180°C/350°F/Gas Mark 4.

1 Pour a glug of olive oil into a frying pan on a medium heat and fry the onion for 4 to 5 minutes.
2 Add the garlic, fry for a further minute and then add all the herbs and spices and the cocoa.
3 Stir in the beef and cook for a few minutes. Keep mixing it so the mince breaks up.
4 Pour in the tomatoes, season with salt and pepper, bring to the boil then turn down the heat and leave to simmer for 10 minutes. If it looks like it is getting too dry, add a little water.
5 When the sauce is nearly ready, take the baking tin and put two round tortillas on top of each other on the lightly oiled base. Tear a third tortilla to fill the corners.
6 Spoon one third of the mix on to the tortilla base. Cover with a tortilla and tear up another one to fill in the corners.
7 Spoon on another third of the mix and cover again with one whole tortilla and one torn up one.
8 Spoon on the final third of the mix and scatter the spring onion on top.
9 Cover with one more tortilla and fill in the corners with the final one.
10 Spread the crème fraîche over the top and cover well with grated cheese.
11 Bake in the oven for 25 to 30 minutes, or until the top is melted and golden.
12 Best served immediately with a green salad.

Serves 4

Preparation time 10 minutes

Cooking time 45–50 minutes

You will need an 8 inch (20cm) square baking tin

Olive oil

1 onion, finely chopped or grated

3 garlic cloves, finely chopped

1 tablespoon ground cumin

1 tablespoon dried oregano

1 teaspoon ground coriander

1 cinnamon stick

Cayenne pepper (optional – we tend to sprinkle on cayenne pepper after the lasagne is served, meaning we can have ours spicy as Archie is not a lover of hot chilli!)

A good pinch of cocoa powder

500g beef mince

400g tin chopped tomatoes

Salt and freshly ground black pepper

9 plain flour tortillas

6–8 spring onions, cut diagonally into 2cm long pieces

300g pot of crème fraîche (half-fat is fine)

2 large handfuls of grated Cheddar cheese

Chicken, leek and tarragon pie with a rosti topping

I used to have an old oven some years ago that just didn't like baking pastry. Somehow, it always used to manage to burn the pastry on the top of a pie and this led me to look for an alternative. This rosti topping was the solution and it works particularly well with this pie, not least because it really does turn the pie into an all-in-one dish. The other thing I am avoiding here is making a white sauce because I think there is already enough cooking needed for this pie. Throwing in a pot of half-fat crème fraîche does the job perfectly.

Preheat your oven to 200°C/400°F/Gas Mark 6.

1 Boil the potatoes for 11 minutes, skin on, in a large covered pan of boiling water. You want the potatoes to be about three-quarters cooked. Take them out of the water and leave to cool.
2 Meanwhile, pour a good glug of olive oil into a pan on a medium heat and cook the onion for 3 to 4 minutes. Add the leek and garlic and cook for a further 2 to 3 minutes and then throw in the chicken and stir for a further minute.
3 Stir in the mustard, then pour in the crème fraîche and simmer gently for a few minutes. Mix in the tarragon, season well with salt and pepper and take the sauce off the heat.
4 Peel the potatoes and grate them coarsely. Melt the butter in a non-metallic bowl in the microwave for 45 seconds (or in a pan on the hob) and mix it well into the grated potatoes so they all get a good covering. You may want to season the potatoes a little at this stage with salt and pepper too.
5 Pour the pie mixture into the dish and sprinkle the grated potato on top.
6 Bake for about 35 minutes until the pie topping is nice and golden and serve immediately.

Serve 4

Preparation time 10 minutes

Cooking time 50 minutes

You will need a 3½ pint (2 litre) pie or baking dish

650g potatoes

Olive oil

1 onion, halved and thinly sliced

2 leeks, trimmed and thickly sliced

1 garlic clove, crushed

4 chicken breasts, cut into good-sized chunks

2 teaspoons wholegrain mustard

300g half-fat crème fraîche

20g tarragon, chopped

Salt and freshly ground black pepper

50g butter

Turbo-quick shepherd's pie

This dish marked a bit of a watershed on the blog. It was when I realised the classics were going to be very popular, especially if they were given the My Daddy Cooks treatment. So here was a very traditional dish, cooked in half quick time, and still coming out delicious. Not only do the sliced potatoes speed up the preparation a little by removing the need to mash them, they also work really well with the meat sauce and crisp up beautifully under the grill. A really firm family favourite.

You will need your oven grill heated to its hottest setting if you are eating immediately. If you are making the pie ahead, you will of course need to reheat it in a conventional oven before you serve it.

1 In a large saucepan, bring some water to the boil and cook the potatoes. They will need about 20 minutes to be cooked, but not too soft to slice. If you are using relatively large potatoes, cut them in half before cooking them.

2 At the same time, heat some oil in a large pan. Cook the lamb mince quickly (2 to 3 minutes).

3 Add the grated onion, garlic and carrot and cook them with the lamb for a further 2 to 3 minutes.

4 Quickly stir the flour in to the meat and vegetables.

5 Splash in the Worcester sauce, add the tomato purée, baked beans and, finally, the water or stock.

6 Bring to the boil then turn down the heat and leave to simmer for 10 to 15 minutes. The sauce will thicken, thanks to the flour. Season it well with salt and pepper.

7 As soon as your potatoes are ready, drain them, cool them down with cold water and slice them into 5mm thick slices. Aesthetics don't matter too much here, you will get a mix of perfect slices and disaster ones.

8 Pour the sauce into a baking dish and cover it with the potato slices (saving the best ones for the top).

9 Grate your Cheddar very generously over the potatoes.

10 Put the pie under a very hot grill until the cheese has melted and is brown and crispy. Serve immediately with green vegetables.

Serves 4

Preparation time 5–10 minutes

Cooking time 30–35 minutes

Approximately 900g smallish potatoes (not new potatoes)

Olive oil

500g lamb mince

1 onion, grated

2 garlic cloves, grated, crushed or finely chopped

1 carrot, finely grated

1 tablespoon plain flour

A very generous dash of Worcester sauce

An equally generous squirt of tomato purée

1 large tin baked beans (we used the reduced salt and sugar ones)

200ml water or beef, chicken or vegetable stock

Salt and freshly ground black pepper

Grated Cheddar cheese

Chicken and cauliflower biryani

There are some things that, try as I might, I simply cannot recreate in the kitchen – and one of them is proper chicken biryani. This is probably mainly due to the fact that real chicken biryani is cooked slowly and meticulously, in several stages and in several pans. For weekday home cooking this method is, to say the least, impractical so it will come as no surprise to you that I cook this delicately spiced dish simply, in one pot on the stove.

Serve with the minty yoghurt raita from the tandoori salmon on page 156.

1   Pour a glug of olive oil into a large heavy-based saucepan on a moderate heat and fry the onion gently for 4 to 5 minutes until it softens.
2   Add the garlic, ginger and all the spices and keep stirring for another minute or so.
3   Throw in the chicken pieces and stir well for a couple of minutes, so they all get nicely coated in the golden colour of the spices and onion.
4   Stir in the cauliflower and the rice, then add the chicken stock. Bring to the boil, cover with tight-fitting lid, turn down the heat and simmer for 10 minutes.
5   Take the dish off the heat and leave it, still with its lid on, for 10 to 15 minutes, or until all the water is absorbed.
6   Stir through the fresh coriander, a squeeze of lemon juice (if using), and serve with the raita.

Serves 4

Preparation time 10 minutes

Cooking time 30–35 minutes

Olive oil

1 onion, halved and thinly sliced

3 garlic cloves, crushed

2.5cm piece of fresh ginger, grated

2 teaspoons ground cumin

2 teaspoons garam masala

½ teaspoon turmeric

1 cinnamon stick

8 boneless chicken thighs and drumsticks, skin removed and cut into large chunks (the easiest way to remove the skin is to pull it off with a sheet of kitchen paper, which helps to grip)

1 small cauliflower, cut into florets

250g basmati rice

650ml chicken stock

A handful of coriander leaves, chopped

Squeeze of lemon juice (optional)

Oven-baked seafood paella

Seeing paellas being slowly and lovingly created in huge paella pans when I was on holiday remains a vivid childhood memory. This paella is made with no less love, but it is somewhat whipped up and then chucked in the oven – and yet the result is no less authentic – especially if you use proper paella rice from the supermarket. It is shorter and fatter than basmati or long-grain rice and will very much add to the authentic feel of the dish. I use a pack of frozen mixed seafood in this recipe because it both helps keep the cost down and makes the paella even quicker to prepare.

Preheat your oven to 180°C/350°F/Gas Mark 4.

1 In an ovenproof pan, heat a good glug of olive oil and cook the onion on a medium heat for 4 to 5 minutes to soften it.
2 Stir in the garlic, red pepper, saffron and tomato purée and cook for a further minute.
3 Pour in the rice and cook for 1 minute, stirring all the time.
4 Add the stock and bring to the boil (I like to have the stock already hot to save time).
5 Give the rice a good stir, cover the dish and put it in the oven.
6 Cook for 15 minutes, stirring once or twice.
7 Add the seafood and the peas, cover again and cook in the oven for a further 10 minutes.
8 Remove from the oven, season with salt and pepper and stir well.
9 Serve straight into bowls, with one lemon wedge for each.

Serves 4

Preparation time 10 minutes

Cooking time 35 minutes

Olive oil

1 onion, finely chopped or grated

3 garlic cloves, finely chopped

1 red pepper, deseeded and sliced into thin strips

A pinch of saffron (if you don't have saffron, you can use turmeric)

A squirt of tomato purée

300g paella rice

1 litre chicken or vegetable stock

350–400g bag of mixed frozen seafood (prawns, mussels, squid), defrosted

2 small handfuls of frozen peas

Salt and freshly ground black pepper

Lemon wedges, to serve

5
Throw It All In (Literally!)

Dishes that require throwing lots of ingredients into one single pot are guaranteed to be popular in my house. Popular with me for the simplicity of their preparation and the reduced washing up they create. Popular with Archie for the scope to generally miss the pan and make plenty of mess. None of which matters as these delicious one-pot recipes are all but impossible to get wrong.

Minty lamb and butternut squash tagine

Ras el hanout is a North African spice mix, which has an infinite number of variations and is what gives many tagines their signature flavour. It is widely available in the spice section of supermarkets and is well worth having in your cupboard as a fallback. Even just sprinkling some on chicken before grilling can make a wonderful difference. In this recipe, it is used classically with lamb (the mint being a slightly unusual addition, but it works so well in this dish). Make sure your lamb is lean and tender. This is not a long-cooking stew and tough meat will not have enough time to be tenderised.

1 Heat a good glug of olive oil in a large heavy-based saucepan on a medium to high heat, throw in the onion and the lamb and fry until the lamb starts to look cooked on the outside.
2 Add the garlic, the tomato purée and the ras el hanout and stir for another minute or so.
3 Pour in the stock and bring it to the boil. Turn down the heat, partially cover the pan and simmer for 25 minutes, then add the butternut squash and cook for a further 20 minutes.
4 With 10 minutes to go, cook the couscous as per the instructions on the packet.
5 When both the lamb and the butternut squash are tender, throw in the chopped mint, season with salt and pepper and serve immediately with the couscous.

Serves 4

Preparation 10 minutes

Cooking time 55 minutes

Olive oil

1 large red onion, halved and finely sliced

450g lamb fillet, neck or leg, cut into small cubes

2 garlic cloves, crushed

1 tablespoon tomato purée

2 teaspoons ras el hanout spice mix

500ml vegetable or lamb stock

1 butternut squash, peeled and cut into cubes

300g couscous

20g mint, leaves chopped

Salt and freshly ground black pepper

Cranberry chops and roasted vegetables

Cranberry sauce is so associated with turkey roast that it may be a surprise to see it here with lamb. It is a great match though and, mixed with the red wine vinegar, it makes for a lovely tangy marinade. I always used to fry or grill my lamb chops, but since I started cooking with Archie, I have become a convert to roasting them. Throwing them in the oven is so much simpler and I actually find it much easier not to overcook them – unlike in the pan where it often seems a little hit and miss to me.

Preheat your oven to 200°C/400°F/Gas Mark 6.

1 Mix the red wine vinegar, the cranberry sauce, rosemary and the garlic in a bowl. Add the lamb chops and cover them well with the marinade.
2 Put all the vegetables in a large rectangular baking dish, drizzle over a really good glug of olive oil, season with some salt and pepper and then bake in the oven for 20 minutes.
3 Take the vegetables out of the oven and make room for the lamb chops. Tuck the tails of the lamb chops around so they make nicely compact round shapes. Put the dish back in the oven for a further 25 to 30 minutes.
4 The lamb is ready when it has taken a nice colour, but is still springy when you press down on it. Serve immediately with mashed potato.

Serves 4

Preparation time 10 minutes

Cooking time 50 minutes

4 tablespoons red wine vinegar

2 tablespoons cranberry sauce

A couple of sprigs of rosemary, stalks removed and leaves chopped finely

2 garlic cloves, crushed

8 lamb loin chops

2 courgettes, cut into moderately chunky 5cm long strips

3 carrots, cut into moderately chunky 5cm long strips

Olive oil

Salt and freshly ground black pepper

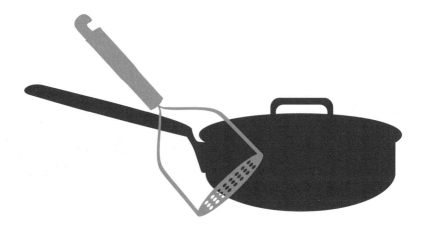

Chicken and tarragon hotpot

In the early days on the blog, I didn't actually have Archie on camera. He was next to me, he could be heard and many of his actions could be seen, but I kept his face out of camera shot. Then he was on the front page of the *London Evening Standard* and we relaxed a bit more about people seeing him – not least because he was asking why he couldn't see his face on the videos! When we came to make this lovely chicken and tarragon hotpot, his speech was suddenly making leaps and bounds and our interaction on that relaxed Sunday afternoon ('What animals eat tarragon, Daddy?') remains one of the best times I have spent with him in the kitchen.

Preheat your oven to around 180°C/350°F/Gas Mark 4.

1 In a casserole dish (with a lid), fry the onion and garlic in some olive oil.
2 When they are nicely soft, add the courgette, carrot and celery and cook them for a few minutes while they soften a little.
3 Add the barley, tarragon and flour, season with salt and pepper and mix well together.
4 Add the chicken and mix again.
5 Layer the potato over the chicken, overlapping the slices and covering the chicken fully.
6 Pour in the stock gently, put the lid on and cook in the oven for approximately 90 minutes.
7 Remove the lid for the last 30 minutes to brown the potatoes a little. When you take the lid off, if you press down gently on the potatoes and see no liquid at all, feel free to add a little water.
8 Serve when the potatoes have browned up nicely.

Serves 4

Preparation time 15 minutes

Cooking time 1½–2 hours

1 onion, chopped

2 garlic cloves, crushed

Olive oil

1 courgette, chopped

2 carrots, chopped

3 sticks of celery, chopped

A good handful of dried pearl barley

25g bunch of tarragon

1 tablespoon plain flour

Salt and freshly ground black pepper

4 chicken drumsticks and 4 chicken thighs

4 potatoes, sliced into 2mm thick slices

700ml good-quality chicken stock

Beef, Guinness and mushroom stew

It's odd because I am not a lover of Guinness as a drink, but I love what it does to a humble beef stew. It tenderises the meat – meaning you can use the cheapest cuts of beef and still have beautifully soft meat – and gives the stew a lovely malty flavour. All the alcohol, of course, disappears during the slow cooking and you are left with a robust and hearty stew, which I always serve with mashed potatoes. Classically this stew is first prepared in a frying pan and then the casserole dish. This all seems like rather too much effort to me so this is the stripped-down version – and it's still delicious!

Not only does this stew freeze brilliantly, it keeps for several days in the fridge and actually probably gets tastier by the day if it is left to chill.

1 Toss the beef in the flour until well coated.
2 Heat the oil in a deep casserole dish and brown the beef briskly. Ideally you would do this in two batches so as not to cram the pan, but for the sake of ease, just do it all in one go.
3 Add the onion, the carrot and the herbs and cook for a further 3 to 4 minutes.
4 Mix in the tomato purée and the mushrooms, cook for a brief minute, and then pour in the Guinness.
5 Bring the casserole to the boil and then simmer, uncovered and very gently, for 2 hours.
6 Once the beef is beyond tender and the sauce rich and thick, season the casserole to your taste and serve with mashed potatoes.

Serves 6

Preparation time 15 minutes

Cooking time 2 hours 15 minutes

750g stewing or braising steak, trimmed of fat and cut into cubes

3 tablespoons plain flour, seasoned with a very generous pinch of salt and freshly ground black pepper

Vegetable oil

1 onion, roughly chopped

1 carrot, roughly chopped

A good handful of whatever fresh herbs you have to have to hand – rosemary, thyme, parsley, bay leaf

2 tablespoons tomato purée

125g button mushrooms, left whole

600ml Guinness or other dark beer

Salt and freshly ground black pepper

School-dinner goulash

There are two things I remember from my school dinners. Sticky treacle sponge pudding and goulash. I loved them both – but not as much as I loved Mrs Knight, our boisterous and warm dinner lady. This simplified version of a classic dish is my little homage to her then, and to extremely happy times at Merry Hill School. The 'secret' ingredient here is the caraway seeds, which add a subtle aniseed touch to the dish. It's no big deal if you don't use them, but they will certainly add something to your dish if you have some to hand.

Preheat your oven to 180°C/350°F/Gas Mark 4.

1 Dust the steak with flour and season well with salt and pepper.
2 Heat a good glug of olive oil in a casserole dish on a medium to high heat and throw in the beef, trying to brown as you stir it for a few minutes (it is not a problem if you don't get it all browned).
3 Add the onion and the garlic and continue to stir for a further minute or so, then add the peppers, the caraway seeds and the paprika.
4 Stir for a short while, then pour in the chopped tomatoes, beef stock and wine, if you are using some.
5 Put the lid on the dish and bake in the oven for somewhere between 2 and 2½ hours.
6 When it is ready to serve, season well with salt and freshly ground pepper, sprinkle with the fresh parsley and serve on plain rice, drizzled with the soured cream.

Serves 4 (with possibly a little over for freezing)

Preparation time 15 minutes

Cooking time 2 hours 15 minutes–2 hours 45 minutes

700g stewing or braising steak

1 tablespoon plain flour

Salt and freshly ground black pepper

Olive oil

1 onion, grated

2 garlic cloves, finely chopped

1 green and 1 red pepper, deseeded and finely sliced

1 teaspoon caraway seeds

2 tablespoons mild paprika

400g tin chopped tomatoes

300ml beef stock

75ml red wine (optional)

Handful of flat-leaf parsley, chopped

150ml soured cream

One-tin roast chicken, new potatoes and asparagus

The great thing about using chicken legs and thighs is that they are such a relatively inexpensive cut of meat and so very easy to cook. The herb and garlic marinade adds a lovely flavour to the chicken pieces and baking them together here with the potatoes, onion and asparagus in one dish makes this the easiest of midweek roasts. This is classic meat and two veg without having to go anywhere near your hob.

Preheat your oven to 200°C/4000°F/Gas Mark 6.

1   In a bowl, mix together the herbs, the garlic, a pinch of salt, some ground pepper and a good drizzle of olive oil. Make two or three slashes with a sharp knife in the skin of each chicken piece, mix them all into the marinade and leave in the fridge until they are ready to be added to the dish.

2   Mix the sliced potato and the sliced onion with a really good glug of olive oil in the baking dish. Season with salt and pepper and bake for 35 minutes.

3   Take the dish out of the oven, give everything a good stir and mix in the asparagus. Lay the chicken pieces on top of the vegetables and cook for a further 25 to 30 minutes until the chicken is fully cooked through and the potatoes are all soft. Serve immediately.

Serves 4

Preparation time 10 minutes

Cooking time 1 hour

You will need a 13inch (33cm) baking dish

A handful of fresh herbs (such as basil or parsley), chopped (or 2 tsp dried herbs)

3 garlic cloves, finely chopped

Salt and freshly ground black pepper

Olive oil

8 chicken thighs and drumsticks, skin left on

750g small new potatoes, cut into 8mm slices

1 red onion, halved and very thinly sliced

200g asparagus (bottoms removed), cut into 2cm long pieces

Easy chicken and apricot casserole

As with so many recipes in this book, there are lots of more complicated and elaborate ways to prepare a dish like this. I like opting for the throw-it-all-in method. Don't worry if the onions are not totally soft when you fry them and it really is not a problem if the chicken doesn't brown brilliantly when you put it in. Let the stock, the gentle spices and the sweet apricots do their job and you will find yourself with a lovely fragrant stew, naturally thickened by the flour you roll the chicken in.

1 In a large dish, heat a glug of olive oil on a medium heat and fry the onion until it begins to soften.
2 While the onion is cooking, roll the chicken portions in the flour to give a light covering.
3 When the onion is ready, mix in the spices and stir for about 20 seconds.
4 Turn the heat up and add the chicken pieces. Stir them around for a couple of minutes so they start to cook and brown a little.
5 Pour in the stock, bring to the boil then lower the heat and simmer for 25 minutes. Add in the apricots and simmer for a further 20 minutes.
6 Five minutes before the casserole is ready, cook your couscous as per the instructions on the packet.
7 Season the casserole with salt and pepper to your taste, stir in the fresh coriander leaves and serve the casserole on the cooked couscous, sprinkling the almonds on top if you wish.

NOTE: I use boned chicken drumsticks and thighs here as I prefer brown meat in this kind of dish. They are often available in supermarkets and your butcher will certainly supply them too. Failing that, it is actually really easy to remove the bone from legs and thighs. Just use a very sharp knife, make a deep incision lengthways through the flesh down to the bone and then gently cut down and around the bone with strokes of the knife. The flesh will easily just come away and allow the bone to be removed.

Serves 4

Preparation time 10 minutes

Cooking time 50 minutes

Olive oil

1 large onion, chopped

8 boneless chicken drumsticks and/or thighs (see Note)

Some flour for dipping

1 teaspoon turmeric

1 teaspoon ground cinnamon

1 teaspoon ground ginger

600ml good-quality chicken stock

250g ready-to-eat dried apricots, cut in half lengthways

250g couscous

Salt and freshly ground black pepper

A bunch of fresh coriander

A sprinkling of chopped almonds (optional)

Pork and fennel casserole

The natural aniseed flavour of the fennel, together with the thyme, is a lovely match for the pork. And pork tenderloin is a very tender, very underrated and relatively cheap cut of meat. All thrown into a pan and ready in 50 minutes.

1 In a large pan on a medium heat, fry the onion and garlic in a glug of olive oil for 4 to 5 minutes.
2 Throw in the pork and continue to stir until all the pieces change colour and are cooked on the outside.
3 Mix in the fennel, then the lemon zest, the chopped tomatoes, paste or purée, sugar, stock and thyme.
4 Bring to the boil, cover the pan then lower the heat and simmer for 40 minutes until the fennel is nice and soft.
5 Just before serving, chop up and mix in the herby bits from the fennel and season with the salt and pepper. I serve this simply, with plain rice.

Serves 4

Preparation time 10 minutes

Cooking time 50 minutes

1 large onion, grated or chopped

3 garlic cloves, chopped

Olive oil

1 whole pork tenderloin (approx 500g), cut into chunks

1 large fennel bulb, cut into very thin slices (don't throw away the herby bits)

Grated zest of 1 lemon

400g tin chopped tomatoes

A dollop of sun-dried tomato paste or a good squirt of tomato purée

A good pinch of sugar

300ml vegetable or chicken stock

The leaves from a small bunch of thyme

Salt and freshly ground black pepper

Oven-baked pork chops with ratatouille and feta

Pork chops are funny things because I just find them so hard to cook right without drying them out. Many a time I have served up chops that would be better used as table tennis bats. After much trial and error, I have decided that baking them in the oven is one of the safest ways of ensuring a moist chop. Keep a close-ish eye on them towards the end of their cooking time – you want them to remain really springy to the touch – and leave them to rest, covered in foil, at the end to ensure that your pork chops are soft and lovely and tender.

Preheat your oven to 220°C/425°F/Gas Mark 7.

1 Throw the courgette, aubergine, peppers, onion and garlic into a deep baking dish, season with salt and pepper, pour in a really good glug of olive oil and toss all the vegetables in it.
2 Cook the vegetables for 25 minutes in the oven, then turn the temperature down to 200°C/400°F/Gas Mark 6.
3 Take the dish out and mix in the tomatoes and basil. Nestle the pork chops in the ratatouille, covering them with some of the vegetables.
4 Crumble the feta cheese over the top of the ratatouille and bake everything for a further 25 minutes, or until the chops are cooked through but still nice and springy to the touch. The key with pork chops is that you can always cook them a little longer if they are slightly undercooked, but you can never go back if you have overcooked them.
5 Remove the dish from the oven, then cover it with aluminium foil for 5 minutes so the pork chops can rest.
6 Serve the pork chops with the ratatouille spooned over them, together with mashed potatoes or boiled new potatoes.

Serves 4

Preparation time 10 minutes

Cooking time 55 minutes

1 large courgette, cut into 2.5cm cubes

1 large aubergine, cut into 2.5cm cubes

1 yellow and 1 red pepper, deseeded and cut into chunks

1 red onion, cut into wedges

2 garlic cloves, roughly chopped

Salt and freshly ground black pepper

Olive oil

400g tin chopped tomatoes

A good handful of basil leaves, chopped (if you don't have fresh basil, simply stir in a tablespoon of mixed dried herbs such as herbes de Provence)

4 thick pork chops (2.5cm), trimmed of excess fat

100g feta cheese

Sticky baked salmon with sesame noodles

As this is a cookbook, I have to bow to convention and actually give an indication of quantities for this marinade. In reality, I never get my spoons out to measure the ingredients in this kind of sauce – especially if Archie is wielding the bottles, as he so loves to do. This marinade will not go wrong, no matter what quantities you put in it. Just think 'dark, thick and sweet' and you will be bang on the right track.

Preheat your oven to 180°C/350°F/Gas Mark 4.

1 In a large roasting tin, mix together the garlic, ginger, the five spice powder, the honey, a good dash of sesame oil and the soy sauce. Roll the peppers, courgette and the salmon in the sauce just so that they are all really well covered.
2 Remove the salmon fillets and reserve them on a plate.
3 Bake the vegetables in the oven for 35 minutes, maybe turning a few times.
4 With 10 minutes to go, make room for the salmon and put it in the roasting tin too (basting it with some of the juices as you go).
5 Cook your noodles as per the packet's instructions. When they are ready, toss in some sesame oil, a few drops of soy sauce and the spring onion.
6 Serve the salmon and vegetables on the noodles with some optional lime to squeeze on too.

Serves 4

Preparation time 5–10 minutes

Cooking time 35 minutes

2 garlic cloves, crushed

1.5cm cube of fresh ginger, grated

3 teaspoons Chinese five spice powder

3 tablespoons honey

Sesame oil

4–5 tablespoons dark soy sauce

2 large red peppers, deseeded and cut lengthways into 8 slices

3 courgettes, cut lengthways into 5mm slices

4 x 150g salmon fillets, skin and grey flesh removed

240g fine noodles

2 spring onions, finely chopped

Lime, to serve (optional)

Oven-baked risotto

If there is one 'fall-back' dish in our house, it is risotto. It was one of the first things that Archie truly loved and it is still what we always make if he is feeling under the weather. I never make the traditional risotto anymore. I just don't have time to supervise a pan and painstakingly add in stock, one ladle at a time. It's so much better to just put it in the oven and forget about it. Even without following the traditional method, this oven-baked version still comes out light and creamy, thanks to the arborio rice. Needless to say, any vegetable you have in your fridge will work with this recipe – and if you have a bottle of white wine to hand, throw a glass in before stage 3 and just let it boil off a little for a couple of minutes.

Preheat your oven to 180°C/350°F/Gas Mark 4.

1 Pour a glug of olive oil into a large ovenproof dish on a medium heat and cook the onion for 4 minutes, followed by the garlic and vegetables for a further 3 minutes,
2 Pour in the rice and mix it in well with the vegetables.
3 Add the stock, bring it to the boil, cover the dish and put it in the oven for 12 minutes.
4 Take the dish out of the oven, give the rice a really good stir and add the chicken pieces. Cover the dish again and put it back in the oven for 8 minutes.
5 Give the risotto another long stir to cream it up a little, mix in the Parmesan and season with salt and pepper to taste.
6 Cover the dish for one last time, leave it to rest for a couple of minutes, then serve the risotto with extra Parmesan.

Serves 4–6

Preparation time 15 minutes

Cooking time 30 minutes

Olive oil

1 onion, finely chopped or grated

2 garlic cloves, chopped

1 large carrot, diced

2 sticks of celery, chopped

1 courgette, chopped

300g arborio rice (or any other type of risotto rice)

900ml good-quality vegetable or chicken stock

2 large chicken breasts, cut into 2cm cubes

50g freshly grated Parmesan cheese, plus extra to serve

Salt and freshly ground black pepper

6

(Almost) No Cooking Required

Cooking doesn't really get any easier than these pasta sauces. Pretty well the only cooking required is the pasta itself. The sauces are prepared cold, in no time at all, and simply stirred into the warm pasta. Only the roast vegetable recipe requires 'cooking' of sorts, but even then it is a simple case of throwing the vegetables into a baking dish in the oven before stirring them into the penne with some goat's cheese a short while later.

No-cook lemon, cream cheese and smoked salmon sauce

I love pasta dishes where the sauce is quicker to make than the pasta itself. That guarantees a meal on the table in under 15 minutes. It can be tricky to buy good-quality smoked salmon at a reasonable price, so I always look out for special offers and multibuys in the supermarket and freeze it. It defrosts so quickly that it can still be used for even the most last minute of suppers.

1 Put a large saucepan of salted water on to boil and cook your pasta according to the instructions on the packet.
2 When the pasta is cooked, save 3 to 4 tablespoons of the cooking water in a cup and then drain the pasta in a colander.
3 Toss the pasta straight back into the saucepan, add back the reserved cooking water and stir in all the other ingredients. The heat of the pasta will cook the sauce for you.
4 Season with a little salt and pepper if you feel it is necessary (remember that the dish will already be quite salty, thanks to the smoked salmon and the saltiness of the pasta cooking water).

Serves 4

Preparation time 5 minutes (plus cooking the pasta)

450g dried pasta (I prefer linguine with this sauce)

200g cream cheese (at room temperature)

150–200g smoked salmon, cut into strips

25g bunch of dill, finely chopped

The rind and juice of 1 lemon

Salt and freshly ground black pepper

No-cook Parma ham carbonara sauce

Yet another more than simple dish, whose flavours work beautifully without the need to cook the sauce at all. Of course, classic carbonara is made with fried pancetta – and you can do the same if you wish – but using Parma ham means the sauce requires no cooking. The heat of the pasta simply cooks it through when it's mixed in.

1 Put a large saucepan of salted water on to boil and cook your pasta according to the instructions on the packet.
2 In a bowl, mix together the ham, the crème fraîche, half the Parmesan and the egg yolks (the easiest way to separate the yolk is to crack an egg onto the palm of your hand and let the egg white 'drain' off through the gaps between your fingers).
3 When the pasta is cooked, drain it in a colander and mix it immediately with the cream sauce, ensuring all the pasta is coated. Serve immediately with the rest of the Parmesan.

Serves 4

Preparation time 5 minutes (plus cooking the pasta)

450g dried fettucine (or similar flat pasta)

100g Parma ham (or similar, such as serrano or Bayonne), cut into thin strips

300ml pot of crème fraîche

50g good-quality freshly grated Parmesan cheese

2 egg yolks

Feta, mint and pea sauce

Mint and feta are two flavours which are just meant to go together. The mint dramatically enhances the natural tanginess of the feta and turns this 'no-cook' sauce into a lovely summery meal. I cheat – but only very slightly – by adding peas here. They are cooked in the pasta water during the last few minutes of the pasta's cooking time and their natural sweetness rounds off this lovely dish beautifully. Needless to say, a little fried bacon or mild chorizo would also work well with this sauce, although adding either of these would mean the sauce is no longer 'no-cook'!

1 Put a large saucepan of salted water on to boil and cook your pasta according to the instructions on the packet.
2 While the pasta is cooking, crumble the feta cheese into a bowl. Mix in the crème fraiche. Chop the leaves of the mint and add them to the mix.
3 With a few minutes remaining for the pasta to cook, add the peas to the saucepan.
4 When the pasta and the peas are both cooked, drain them and return them immediately to the saucepan so they stay hot. Mix in the feta, cream and mint sauce. You will need to stir the pasta really well so the feta starts to melt nicely.
5 Season with salt and pepper if you wish. Go gently with the salt as the feta already has quite a salty taste.
6 If you would like a little extra sharpness to your sauce, squeeze in a little lemon juice before serving the pasta with lots of freshly grated parmesan

Serves 4

Preparation time 5 minutes
(plus cooking the pasta)

450g tagliatelle or any long dried pasta

200g feta cheese

**200g crème fraiche
(half-fat is fine)**

**Approximately 25g
fresh mint**

200g frozen peas

**Salt and freshly ground
black pepper**

**A squeeze of fresh lemon
juice (optional)**

**Freshly grated Parmesan
cheese, to serve**

No-cook cherry tomato, basil and garlic pasta sauce

If ever there was a 'cheat's' pasta, this has to be it! The 'no-cook' element of this is an understatement because the sauce actually takes on all its flavour in the fridge. Still, I always find it hugely gratifying – and reassuring – that a meal so tasty can be so simple and require such little effort. It's worth using a really good quality extra virgin olive oil for this dish because it will greatly enhance the flavour.

1 Put a large saucepan of salted water on to boil and cook your pasta according to the instructions on the packet.
2 Add the tomato, garlic and basil to a sealable plastic food bag. Add a very good pinch of salt and some ground pepper.
3 Finally, pour in a really good glug of olive oil. You don't want the ingredients to be absolutely drowning in oil but, at the same time, you don't want them to be dry.
4 Seal the bag and put it aside while the pasta cooks.
5 When the pasta is cooked, drain it and return it immediately to the saucepan so it doesn't lose too much of its heat.
6 Toss in the sauce from the plastic bag and mix well. Add a little olive oil if the pasta looks a touch dry.
7 Season with extra salt and pepper, if necessary, and serve straight away, finishing off with lots of fresh Parmesan.

Serves 4

Preparation time 5 minutes
(plus cooking the pasta)

450g dried spaghetti

300g cherry tomatoes,
cut into quarters

2 garlic cloves, finely
chopped

60g basil, leaves chopped

Salt and freshly ground
black pepper

Lots of good-quality extra
virgin olive oil

Freshly grated Parmesan
cheese, to serve

Pesto sauce

Home-made pesto is so easy to make and much more satisfying than when bought in a jar. There are literally hundreds of combinations to make pesto so don't worry too much about the quantities. It will be delicious however you make it. When I make pesto for pasta, I always stir a little bit of the pasta's cooking water into the sauce as it helps loosen it up a little.

1 Put a large saucepan of salted water on to boil and cook your pasta according to the instructions on the packet.
2 In a food mixer or blender, blend together the garlic, pine nuts, basil leaves, salt and cheese. If you don't have a mixer or blender, this can be done in a pestle and mortar.
3 Stir in the olive oil – and a few tablespoons of the cooking water – and your pesto sauce is ready.
4 Drain the pasta and stir in the pesto sauce.
   If you want the pasta to be a little hotter, return it briefly to the heat, stirring to ensure is doesn't stick.
6 Serve with lots of fresh Parmesan.

Serves 4

Preparation time 10 minutes (plus cooking the pasta)

450g dried tagliatelle

3 garlic cloves

50g pine nuts

60g basil, leaves removed

A good pinch of sea salt or rock salt

25g freshly grated Parmesan cheese, plus extra to serve

25g freshly grated Pecorino cheese (or another 25g Parmesan)

150ml olive oil

Roast vegetable and goat's cheese penne

Not quite a 'no-cook' pasta because these vegetables are baked in the oven, but this dish certainly requires no work over the hob. I always make double the quantity of these sweet roasted vegetables because they can be reinvented for any number of uses for lunch the following day – in sandwiches, couscous salads or served with hummus. You'll need a creamy, rindless goat's cheese to finish this pasta off with.

Preheat your oven to 200°C/400°F/Gas Mark 6.

1 In a large baking dish, mix together all the vegetables, the olive oil, the balsamic vinegar and the honey.
2 Roast the vegetables for 45 minutes, stirring them well every 15 minutes or so.
3 With 15 minutes to go, cook the penne in boiling salted water and drain when cooked.
4 Add the goat's cheese to the vegetables and stir the penne into the baking dish itself. The heat of the pasta and the vegetables will melt the cheese.
5 Season with salt and pepper if necessary and serve immediately.

Serves 4

Preparation time 10 minutes (plus 45 minutes to cook the vegetables)

2 red peppers, sliced into 1cm strips

1 yellow pepper, sliced into 1cm strips

2 red onions, halved and sliced

1 aubergine, roughly cut into 2cm chunks

1 courgette, roughly cut into 1cm cubes

3 garlic cloves, chopped

5 tablespoons olive oil

3 tablespoons balsamic vinegar

A long drizzle of honey (2–3 tablespoons)

450g penne pasta

125g soft goat's cheese, crumbled

Salt and freshly ground black pepper

7
Wok on the Wild Side

Poetic licence here as only two of these recipes
actually use a wok, but I loved the title too much
not to use it! And while none of them are particularly
wild either, all these dishes are cooked on the hob,
requiring more vigilance if you have little helpers in
the kitchen. The hob is the only heat you will find in
these recipes. There are some curries in this chapter
but I use warm spices like cumin and coriander for
them and none of these dishes are hotly spiced in
any way at all.

Creamy pork and cider

It is traditional for this dish from Normandy to be cooked with a dash of Calvados, which is then flambéed. Much as Archie would find this part of the preparation highly entertaining to say the least, I choose to leave it out! You still get the rich apple flavour thanks to the cider (all the alcohol, of course, disappears during the cooking) – and you get the double bonus of having enough for the adults to drink at the table too!

1 Heat the butter and a good drizzle of olive oil in a large pan on a medium heat and cook the onion for 4 to 5 minutes until it starts to soften.
2 Add the pork pieces and continue to stir for 3 to 4 minutes.
3 Throw in the apple and cook for a further minute or so.
4 Pour in the cider and scrape any bits off the base of the pan.
5 Simmer for about 10 minutes so the pork cooks through and the cider reduces a little.
6 Right at the end, mix in the crème fraîche and the mustard and let it bubble gently for a minute or two. You want the sauce to slightly thicken. If it looks a touch liquid, simply cook it for a little longer.
7 Season with salt and pepper, sprinkle on the chopped parsley and serve immediately with mashed potatoes and green beans.

Serves 4

Preparation time 10 minutes

Cooking time 20 minutes

A small knob of butter

Olive oil

1 onion, finely chopped

500g pork tenderloin, cut into 2.5cm cubes

1 large or 2 small firm apples (such as Cox's or Braeburn), cored and cut into 12–16 wedges, skin on

275ml good-quality cider

75ml (3 generous tablespoons) crème fraîche (half-fat is fine)

1 teaspoon Dijon mustard

Salt and freshly ground black pepper

Chopped flat-leaf parsley, to serve

Thai minced chicken with basil

This dish (*gai pad grapao*) is a classic, which you will find in any Thai restaurant. It is extremely quick to make and doesn't require a long list of hard-to-come-by ingredients. Traditionally you would use holy basil, but this is nearly impossible to find anywhere other than in specialist stores. Normal sweet basil actually works just as well here, although the authenticity does take a slight hit. If you can't find minced chicken, you can just as easily use minced beef, turkey or pork, and this also works well as a vegetarian dish, using steamed broccoli, cauliflower florets and grated carrot.

1 Cook your rice according to the instructions on the packet.
2 If you have a pestle and mortar, crush together the garlic, shallot and chilli.
3 With 6 to 7 minutes left for your rice to cook, heat up a wok on a high heat and pour in a good drizzle of the oil.
4 Drop in the garlic, shallot and chilli. They will sizzle and cook very quickly.
5 Before the garlic has time to go brown, mix in the chicken mince. Keep stirring until it is all cooked and broken up and any liquid has evaporated away.
6 Mix in the sugar, the fish sauce and finally the basil.
7 Serve immediately on the jasmine rice, with some green vegetables if you want.

Serves 4

Preparation time 5 minutes

Cooking time 15 minutes

250g jasmine rice

3 garlic cloves, finely chopped

2 shallots, finely grated

2 fresh green chillies, deseeded and chopped very finely

Vegetable oil

500g minced chicken

1–2 teaspoons palm sugar or light muscovado sugar

3 tablespoons Thai fish sauce

50g basil, leaves torn up

Mediterranean fish stew

This was a tricky recipe to write because I am not sure my fish stew ever comes out the same twice. This is good news, though, because it means the ingredients are pretty interchangeable (for the fish, I simply buy whatever I can find on special offer) and, no matter how you throw it all together, it somehow always works. So here is my current fish stew recipe – until I make the next one! Unlike many other recipes, the saffron should not be replaced by turmeric. It's worth getting for this stew as it really does enhance both its flavour and colour.

1 Heat a good glug of olive oil in a large saucepan and soften the onion, garlic and fennel on a low to medium heat for 10 minutes.
2 Pour in the tomatoes, wine, stock, saffron, the thyme and the bay leaf. Bring to the boil then lower the heat and simmer for 20 minutes.
3 Gently add the fish and prawns and cook for a further 6 minutes. Season to taste.
4 Throw in the herby tops of the fennel and serve with new potatoes, green vegetables and the lemon wedges. When I am feeling particularly lazy, I love serving this on its own with loads of fresh bread.

Serves 4

Preparation time
10–15 minutes

Cooking time 40 minutes

Olive oil

1 large onion, finely chopped

4 garlic cloves, finely chopped

1 large fennel bulb, chopped (keep the herby tops for serving)

400g tin chopped tomatoes

150ml dry white wine

200ml fish stock or water

A good pinch of saffron strands

1 tablespoon fresh thyme

1 bay leaf

500g any firm white fish fillets (sea bass, cod, pollock), cut into 4–5 cm chunks

150g peeled raw tiger prawns (you can also simply use 600g white fish if you don't have prawns)

Salt and freshly ground black pepper

1 lemon, cut into quarters, to serve

Creamy prawn curry

Much as I would love to be telling you that I have seen this very same curry cooked on the beaches of Goa, I have never even come close to visiting that paradise. Still, this is my take on the classic Goan prawn curry. It's a dish I love to cook because it is just so simple to put together and the ingredients produce a wonderfully bitter sweet, slightly tangy curry. Traditionally you would use tamarind paste, but there is no need to go to the extra expense of buying it – lemon juice is a more than adequate substitute. This recipe specifically uses creamed coconut, which is available in most supermarkets and comes in the form of a hard block. It is a mixture of both the coconut milk and the coconut flesh and it is important not to use coconut milk here because you will lose the sweetness that the flesh in the coconut cream gives the dish.

1 Cook the rice according to the instructions on the packet.
2 Meanwhile, heat a glug of oil in a large pan on a medium heat, pour in the onion, garlic and ginger and keep stirring them for 4 to 5 minutes until everything has started to soften.
3 Mix in the powdered spices and cinnamon stick and cook for a further minute.
4 Add 300ml water and the creamed coconut and stir it so the coconut 'melts' into the pan.
5 Bring to the boil then lower the heat and simmer for a few minutes so the sauce thickens slightly, then stir in the lemon juice.
6 Drop in the prawns and cook for a further 4 to 5 minutes, until the prawns are pink and cooked through.
7 Check the thickness of the sauce. It is unlikely to look too liquid but, if it does, cook it for a further minute or so. If it has thickened too much, simply drizzle in some water.
8 Remove the cinnamon stick, season to taste and serve the curry immediately with the rice and some mango chutney.

Serves 4

Preparation time 5 minutes

Cooking time 15 minutes

250g basmati rice

Vegetable or sunflower oil

1 onion, finely chopped or grated

1 garlic clove, crushed

2.5cm cube of fresh ginger, grated

2 teaspoons ground coriander

A good pinch of turmeric

Pinch of chilli powder (optional, but recommended)

1 cinnamon stick

150g creamed coconut

Juice of ½ lemon

500g frozen peeled raw prawns, defrosted

Salt and freshly ground black pepper

Mango chutney, to serve

Thai vegetable green curry

Thai green curry definitely falls into the category of dishes of which you may say, 'Why don't I just buy the sauce from a supermarket?' It's a fair point, but once you see how quick and easy it is to make the paste (and how much fresher it tastes), you will see why I really do recommend making your own. The paste also freezes brilliantly well, so double, triple or even quadruple the quantities and you have prepared ahead for the easiest meals you could possibly make.

The big unknown quantity with any green curry paste is the amount of green chillies to put in. I have seen recipes range from 3 to 15 (which seems, I must admit, somewhat foolhardy!) I would suggest a good starting point is three green chillies – you can always increase the quantities next time round if you find it too mild. This recipe will work equally well with chicken or prawns, either with the vegetables or instead of them.

1 Cook the rice according to the instructions on the packet.
2 Meanwhile, blitz all the paste ingredients in a food mixer until you get a pesto-like consistency.
3 Heat the oil in a frying pan on a medium heat and cook the squash for 5 to 6 minutes or until it starts to soften a little.
4 Add the mushrooms and cook for a further 2 minutes.
5 Add in 4 tablespoons of the green curry paste and mix it well, then add the coconut milk and stock.
6 Bring the sauce to the boil, then turn down the heat and leave it to simmer for 10 minutes.
7 Add in the asparagus pieces and the mange tout and cook for a further 5 minutes, until all the vegetables are nice and soft. If your rice seems to be ready before the curry, simply drain it in a colander and cover it with a dry kitchen cloth while the curry finishes off for a few minutes.
8 Right at the end, mix in some fresh coriander leaves and serve the curry on the jasmine rice with the lime wedges.

Serves 4

Preparation time 15–20 minutes

Cooking time 25 minutes

250g jasmine rice

Vegetable or groundnut oil

1 butternut squash, peeled and cut into chunks

100g button mushrooms

1 tin coconut milk

350ml vegetable stock

250g asparagus (bottoms removed), cut into 2cm pieces

150g mange tout

Lime wedges, to serve

For the green curry paste:
3 lemon grass stalks (hard outer layer removed)

2.5cm cube of fresh ginger, peeled

3 green chillies

4 garlic cloves

2 shallots

50g coriander, plus extra to serve

2 pieces of lime rind

1 tablespoon Thai fish sauce

1 teaspoon ground coriander

A small drizzle of vegetable or groundnut oil

Roast tomato and squid capellini

I am a huge fan of squid (and, to my relative surprise, Archie has loved it since the first time we gave it to him), but it can divide opinions. Although it is relatively cheap and extremely easy to prepare, I think two things generally put people off squid. Firstly, it can be a little, how best to put this, squishy when raw (those of you who are more direct may call it slimy!) Secondly, it can come out very tough and chewy when cooked. Well, as long as long as the squid tubes are cleaned at the fish counter or fishmonger (or bought frozen), they are far from slimy. And if the squid is cooked correctly (i.e. very quickly), it is extremely tender and surprisingly sweet. I think it is worth the extra time (although very little effort indeed) required to roast the tomatoes because it really intensifies their flavour. They can even be made hours or a few days in advance and stored in the fridge. Feel free to throw in some chorizo if you have some to hand and if you really can't bring yourself to eat the squid, the tomatoes make a fabulous, deep Napolitana sauce on their own.

Preheat your oven to 160°C/325°F/Gas Mark 3.

1 On a baking tray, drizzle some olive oil, spread the chopped garlic and then place the vine tomatoes on top. Drizzle another healthy glug of olive oil over the tomatoes, season with a little salt and pepper and cook in the oven for 35 minutes.
2 With approximately 10 minutes to go (it will depend on the stated cooking time on the pasta packet), cook the capellini in salted boiling water.
3 Take the tomatoes out of the oven, remove the vines and transfer them to a bowl, scraping all the oil and garlic with you.
4 Heat a frying pan, add some olive oil and cook the squid on a high heat for no more than a minute.
5 Stir in the tomatoes and parsley and add the pasta as soon as it is drained. Season and serve with the Parmesan.

Serves 4

Preparation time 10 minutes

Cooking time 40 minutes

Olive oil

3 garlic cloves, chopped

300g tomatoes on the vine

Salt and freshly ground black pepper

450g dried capellini (or any other thin pasta)

400g squid tubes, cleaned by the fishmonger and cut into 1cm rings

1 tablespoon chopped flat-leaf parsley

Freshly grated Parmesan cheese, to serve

Spinach, salmon and cherry tomato linguine

Archie used to call this 'traffic light pasta', for obvious reasons. It is a colourful and zingy dish, where the sauce needs to not be overcooked or else the cherry tomatoes lose their shape and sweetness. Italian friends of mine say that you should never serve Parmesan with a fish pasta, and who am I to argue with them? Except that I really do recommend serving lots of Parmesan with this dish!

1 Put a large saucepan of salted water on to boil and cook your pasta according to the instructions on the packet.
2 Meanwhile, heat the olive oil in a frying pan on a medium to high heat and cook the red onion for 3 to 4 minutes.
3 Add the garlic, lemon zest and salmon and cook for 3 more minutes.
4 Add a few tablespoons of the cooking water to the pan. Mix in the spinach, keep stirring and let it wilt.
5 Finally, stir in the cherry tomatoes and season with salt and pepper. Cook for 1 more minute and then take the sauce off the heat.
6 Drain the pasta and mix it into the sauce.
7 Pour in the lemon juice and a final glug of olive oil and mix very well together.
8 Leave the pasta to 'rest' for a few minutes so that the pasta absorbs the lemony flavour, then serve with lots of fresh Parmesan.

Serves 4

Preparation time 10-15 minutes

Cooking time 15 minutes

450g dried linguine

2 tablespoons olive oil, plus extra to serve

1 red onion, cut in half and thinly sliced

2 garlic cloves, chopped

Grated zest of 1 lemon

2 x 150g salmon fillets, skin and grey flesh removed and cut into 2cm cubes

400g fresh spinach or 300g frozen spinach, defrosted

250g cherry tomatoes, left whole

Salt and freshly ground black pepper

Juice of ½ lemon

Freshly grated Parmesan cheese, to serve

Simple chicken and spinach curry

Archie doesn't like hot curries, so I am always looking for ways of cooking warm and mild curries. Cumin, turmeric and coriander are all gentle spices and the fresh spinach goes particularly well with the gravy they create. I add ½ teaspoon chilli powder just to give the curry a little extra depth, but it certainly doesn't make it hot. Unlike Archie, Jo and I do like our curries to have a big kick, but we can easily satisfy our love of heat by sprinking some extra chilli powder on our portions.

1 Heat the oil in a large saucepan and fry the onion until it starts to go golden.
2 Add the ginger and garlic, stir for about a minute, then add the spices and salt and stir for a further 2 minutes.
3 Add the chicken and keep stirring well for 5 to 6 minutes. If the dish looks like it is getting too dry, add a splash of water.
4 Squirt in some tomato purée, throw in the spinach and continue to stir for a couple of minutes.
5 Add in a few more tablespoons of water, cover the saucepan, bring to the boil then turn down the heat and simmer on a very low heat for 30 minutes. Check the curry half way through. If it is looking a little dry, add a little extra water. If the sauce is a little bit too liquid at the end, simply cook the curry, uncovered, for a few minutes so the excess can evaporate.
6 Serve with basmati rice or simply with naan bread or any similar flatbread.

Serves 4

Preparation time 15 minutes

Cooking time 45–50 minutes

Vegetable oil

2 onions, finely chopped

2.5cm piece of fresh ginger, grated

2 large garlic cloves, finely chopped

2 teaspoons ground cumin

2 teaspoons ground coriander

A small pinch of turmeric

A small pinch of chilli powder (about ½ teaspoon)

A pinch of salt

8 chicken thighs or drumsticks, skin removed (the easiest way to remove the skin is to pull it off with a sheet of kitchen paper, which helps to grip)

1 tablespoon tomato purée

700g fresh spinach or 400g frozen spinach, defrosted

Minced lamb and pea curry

This is such a lovely dish. The yoghurt, tomatoes and spices gently cook the lamb mince, leaving it so tender and succulent. As most of the liquid is simmered away, the lamb ends up with more of a shepherd's pie-type consistency, proving that not all great curries need a great sauce. Although bursting with flavour, this is definitely a mild curry, but you can spice it up with extra green chillies if you like.

1 In a good-sized frying pan on a medium heat, heat a glug of oil and fry the onion for 5 minutes until it is golden.
2 Mix in all the spices, the chilli, the garlic and the ginger and continue to fry for a few minutes.
3 Add the minced lamb and cook it with the onion, breaking it up with your spoon as you stir.
4 Once the lamb is no longer raw, add the yoghurt, one tablespoon at a time, giving it a few seconds each time to get fully absorbed.
5 Pour in the tomatoes and a pinch of salt, bring to the boil then turn down the heat and let the lamb simmer on a low heat for about 20 minutes. If the sauce looks like it is getting a little too dry, add a little water.
6 With 5 minutes cooking time remaining, throw in the peas.
7 Serve with plain basmati rice or simply with Indian flatbreads.

Serves 4

Preparation time 10 minutes

Cooking time 35 minutes

Vegetable oil

1 large onion, finely chopped or grated

1 teaspoon ground coriander

1 teaspoon turmeric

1 teaspoon ground cumin

1 mild fresh green chilli, deseeded and finely chopped

2 garlic cloves, chopped

2.5cm cube of fresh ginger, grated

600g lamb mince

1 small pot (approx 150g) of natural yoghurt

1 small tin chopped tomatoes (or ½ large one)

A pinch of salt

Two handfuls of frozen peas, defrosted

Mild lentil curry with cauliflower

Lentils lend themselves so well to being stewed in spices and the result is this very warming and comforting dish. To make this curry a little more filling, I have added cauliflower and carrot, meaning that this curry really is a whole meal in its own right. Traditionally dhals, or lentil curries, are made in two separate dishes, one to fry the onions and spices, another to stew the lentils. I have simplified the dish here and you will only need one large saucepan or deep frying pan. Feel free to add or substitute whatever vegetables you happen to have in the fridge, although if you are adding particularly absorbent ones such as potatoes, you may want to use a little extra water.

This dhal is best eaten with chapatis or flatbreads, but can equally be served on plain rice.

1 Rinse the lentils well in a sieve under cold water.
2 In a large saucepan or deep frying pan, fry the onion in a glug of vegetable oil on a medium heat for 4 minutes, then add the garlic and ginger and cook for a further minute. Now, add the turmeric, garam masala, and chilli and a pinch of salt and stir for a further minute.
3 Stir in the carrot and cook for a further 2 minutes, then add the lentils, pour in 750ml water and bring to the boil (you may want to spoon off a little of the froth that comes to the surface).
4 Cover the pan, then turn down the heat and simmer for 20 minutes, then take the lid off and add the cauliflower. Simmer for a further 10 to 15 minutes, stirring from time to time, until the water is absorbed and the cauliflower is soft.
5 Season with a little extra salt if you feel the dhal needs it and serve with the lemon wedges.

Serves 4-6

Preparation time 10 minutes

Cooking time 45 minutes

250g red lentils

1 large onion, cut in half and thinly sliced

Vegetable oil

2 garlic cloves, chopped

1.5cm cube of fresh ginger, grated

1 teaspoon turmeric

2 teaspoons garam massala

A small pinch of chilli powder (or more, depending on your family's spice threshold)

Salt

1 large carrot, diced

200g cauliflower, cut into very small florets

Lemon wedges, to serve

Sausage jambalaya

I love it when a ridiculously glamorous name masks a ridiculously simple dish. This is basically rice simmered in chopped tomatoes, brought to life by the flavour of the chorizo and the chipolata sausages. Jambalaya is a creole word from New Orleans, literally meaning 'all jumbled up'. That means that this dish can just as easily be made with chicken, prawns, salmon or, in reality, anything you may have to hand. If you want to cook this as a simple spice-free dish, it still works really well without the chilli.

1 In a large frying pan, heat a good glug of olive oil on a medium heat. Cook the chipolatas until they start to brown, then add the chorizo and cook for a further 90 seconds, while the chorizo releases red oils.
2 Add the onion, green chilli, celery and garlic, stirring for 2 minutes, then add the green and red peppers.
3 Continue to stir everything for a further minute, then pour in the long-grain rice, mixing it well with all the other ingredients in the pan.
4 Throw in the tomatoes, the stock, a dash of Worcester sauce and the Tabasco, if you are using it.
5 Cover, bring to the boil and simmer for 30 minutes until all the liquid has been absorbed. Check the pan from time to time to make sure you don't need to add a little water if the rice is getting too dry.
6 When the rice is cooked, give it a really good stir. This will help mix in any remaining pieces of tomato that haven't been absorbed. Season to taste and serve immediately.

Serves 4

Preparation time 10–15 minutes

Cooking time 45 minutes

Olive oil

12 good-quality pork chipolatas, cut into 3 pieces

100g cooking chorizo, sliced into 1cm thick pieces

1 onion, finely chopped or grated

1 green chilli, deseeded and chopped

2 sticks of celery, chopped

2 garlic cloves, chopped

1 green pepper, deseeded and chopped into small squares

1 red pepper, deseeded and chopped into small squares

300g long-grain rice

400g tin chopped tomatoes

600ml chicken or vegetable stock

A dash of Worcester sauce

An optional dash of Tabasco (very much depending on your family's spice threshold)

Salt and freshly ground black pepper

Quick sesame beef chow mein

Wok cooking has the big advantage of being extremely quick, but it is not always ideal for cooking with younger kids. This doesn't stop Archie helping though. Simple things like passing me the ingredients keep him well occupied while I cook over the high heat. Preparing the cooked noodles by chopping them up for me is another favourite of his.

It is important to maintain the very high heat in the wok by not crowding it with too much food.

1 Mix the beef with a really good dash of soy sauce, the five spice powder, the cornflour and the sesame seeds.
2 Cook the noodles according to the instructions on the packet, then drain and cool them with cold running water. Toss in a little sesame oil to stop them from sticking together.
3 Using scissors or a knife, cut the noodles into shorter strands.
4 Heat the wok on a high heat until it starts to smoke and pour in the vegetable or groundnut oil.
5 Pour in the beef and cook for 1½ minutes until all the pieces have changed colour and are seared on the outside.
6 Add the red pepper and fry for a further minute, then the carrot for 30 seconds and finally the bean sprouts for a final minute.
7 Mix in the chopped noodles, another dash of soy sauce (to turn the noodles dark) and a final drizzle of sesame oil and serve immediately.

Serves 4

Preparation time 10 minutes

Cooking time 10 minutes

400g tender steak, thinly sliced (this dish certainly does not need expensive fillet – a cut such as sirloin will work very well)

Dark soy sauce

A good pinch of Chinese five spice powder

1 tablespoon cornflour

A large sprinkling of sesame seeds

250g egg noodles

Sesame oil

2 tablespoons vegetable or groundnut oil

1 red pepper, deseeded and finely sliced

1 small carrot, finely grated

125g bean sprouts

8
Foolproof Grills and Bakes

Time to let your oven take the strain. Over half of these dishes take less than 30 minutes from start to finish and nearly all of them require no use of the hob at all. I particularly love meals which use the oven, not least because Archie and I often have our greatest fun and messiest quality time in the kitchen together while we wait for something to cook.

Toad in the hole

You'd have to go a long way to find a more comforting dish than toad in the hole. As Archie can virtually inhale Yorkshire puddings and is a sausage fiend too, I think that food doesn't get much more appealing for him than this. As this dish involves plenty of wrapping, mixing and mess, it's also a great recipe to make with kids.

If you're not up for making the onion gravy, this toad in the hole is just as tasty with a dollop of tomato or onion chutney or even tomato ketchup. Although traditionally served with mash, we have been known to serve it with just some steamed greens or a bit of salad.

Preheat your oven to 220°C/425°F/Gas Mark 7.

1 Wrap the sausages with the bacon and put them in a deep baking dish. Drizzle them with a little vegetable oil. You want the base to have a good covering of oil too.
2 Bake the sausages for 20 minutes until the bacon starts to go nice and crispy.
3 While the sausages are baking, sift the flour and salt into a bowl, drop in the egg and whisk in the milk. Try not to over-whisk the batter, but you will want it to be nice and smooth.
4 Remove the sausages from the oven. Be careful as the oil will be very hot. Pour the batter into the dish and swirl it around the sausages.
5 Bake the toad in the hole for a further 25 to 30 minutes. Whatever you do, don't open the oven for at least 20 minutes. The toad in the hole is ready when the batter has risen and is golden brown.

NOTE: To make the onion gravy while the sausages are cooking, fry the onion gently in a drizzle of oil in a non-stick frying pan on a moderate heat for about 15 minutes. Add the sugar and stir for a few more minutes. Stir in the flour and keep stirring until all the flour is absorbed. Pour in the stock and bring it to the boil. Let the sauce simmer gently for 5 minutes until it has thickened slightly. Season before serving.

Serves 4

Preparation time 10 minutes

Cooking time 50 minutes

For the 'toad':
8 thick pork sausages (using excellent quality sausages will dramatically improve this dish)

8 rashers of streaky bacon

A large glug of vegetable oil

For the 'hole':
100g plain flour

A pinch of salt

1 egg

300ml milk

For the optional onion gravy:
2 onions, thinly sliced

Olive oil

A good pinch of brown sugar

1 tablespoon plain flour

500ml beef stock (preferably) or vegetable stock

Salt and freshly ground black pepper

Parmesan breaded chicken with paprika potato wedges

When I was a kid, breaded chicken was one of my absolute favourite meals. Times have changed since then, however, and deep-frying pieces of chicken is no longer so appealing. It is also much less practical when there is a little helper around. Oven baking the chicken actually works really well, the light coating of oil being more than enough to crisp up the breadcrumbs. Serve this with paprika potato wedges for an extremely moreish midweek treat.

Preheat your oven to 220°C/425°F/Gas Mark 7.

1 Mix together the breadcrumbs and Parmesan. Season the flour with salt and pepper.
2 Pat the chicken pieces dry with some kitchen paper. Dip each one in the flour, shake off any excess, then dip it in the egg and finally roll it in the breadcrumb mix. Set the chicken pieces aside and prepare the potatoes.
3 In a bowl, mix the potatoes with a good drizzle of olive oil, a dusting of paprika, salt and pepper, then lay them out on a baking tray and put in the oven.
4 After the potatoes have been cooking for 10 minutes, pour some olive oil into a shallow baking dish. You basically want just enough to cover the base of the dish. Put the dish in the oven for 5 minutes.
5 Take the dish out of the oven and put the chicken pieces in. Turn them over with a fork, so they all get a really good covering of the hot oil.
6 Bake the chicken in the oven for 30 minutes. Check the chicken pieces after 15 minutes. If there is excessive oil and liquid in the base of the dish, take it out of the oven and remove the liquid using a spoon. If for any reason your potatoes race ahead and cook too quickly, simply cover them with some aluminium foil.
7 Serve the chicken pieces straight out of the oven when they have crisped up, with the potatoes, lemon wedges and some green vegetables.

Serves 4

Preparation time 20 minutes

Cooking time 45 minutes

100g breadcrumbs

50g freshly grated Parmesan cheese (or just replace the cheese with some extra breadcrumbs)

A wide bowl filled with a good layer of plain flour

Salt and freshly ground black pepper

8 large chicken drumsticks or thighs, skin removed (the easiest way to remove the skin is to pull it off with a sheet of kitchen paper, which helps to grip)

1 egg (be aware you may need a second one), whisked in a bowl

Lemon wedges, to serve

For the paprika potato wedges:
3 potatoes, each cut into 8 wedges, skin on

Olive oil

Mild paprika

Salt and freshly ground black pepper

Mozzarella and tomato penne pasta bake

This is an oven-baked version of the classic Italian Caprese salad of mozzarella, basil and tomato. I add a good chunk of fresh Parmesan too, giving the dish a little more zip. You can always throw in any sun-dried tomatoes you may have to hand and feel free to add any cooked meats. If you are really rushed for time, you can miss out the oven part of the dish completely and simply stir the other ingredients into the hot pasta on a low heat and allow the cheese to melt. Personally, I find there is something very comforting about serving and eating pasta bakes and so I much prefer eating this dish out of the oven.

Preheat your oven to 180°C/350°F/Gas Mark 4.

1 Put a large saucepan of salted water on the boil and cook your pasta according to the instructions on the packet.
2 When cooked, drain the pasta but don't cool it down in cold water. Mix in the mozzarella (holding back a handful), the tomatoes, the basil, half the Parmesan and some salt and pepper.
3 Sprinkle with the remaining Parmesan and mozzarella and bake in the oven for 15 to 20 minutes or until the mozzarella is melted and the Parmesan cheese is golden.

Serves 4

Preparation time barely a few minutes

Cooking time 30–35 minutes

400g dried penne, or any other pasta shape

300g mozzarella, grated

400g tin chopped tomatoes

A good handful of basil leaves, chopped

100g freshly grated Parmesan cheese

Salt and freshly ground black pepper

Olive oil

Turkey and cranberry meatloaf

This turkey meatloaf makes a real change from the classic beef meatloaf and it is absolutely scrumptious. Turkey and cranberry are such a classic flavour combination that it makes sense to use them here. As with all meatloaves, this one is actually great when cold and is at its finest in a lunchtime sandwich. That is why I have made this meatloaf a little larger than is possibly needed for a family of four – although it is so moreish that it may not actually make it to the next day!

Preheat your oven to 180°C/350°F/Gas Mark 4.

1 Line a large loaf tin with greaseproof paper (grease the tin with a little oil to help the paper stick).
2 Mix together all the ingredients except the cranberry jelly and press the mixture into the loaf tin.
3 Melt the cranberry sauce for 20 seconds or until it becomes liquid in the microwave (or in a pan on the hob) and glaze the top of the meatloaf using a pastry brush (or your hands, as long as the sauce has cooled down).
4 Bake in the oven for about an hour, until it is fully cooked through.
5 Serve with mashed potatoes and extra cranberry sauce.

Serves 4, with possibly extra for sandwiches

Preparation 10 minutes

Cooking time 1 hour

650g turkey mince

1 small onion, finely chopped or grated

2 sticks of celery, finely chopped

100g sage and onion (or similar) stuffing mix

100g dried cranberries

2 eggs

A few drops of milk

3 tablespoons cranberry jelly, plus extra for serving

Gammon steaks with pea mash

Gammon steak is so easy to grill and is pretty flavoursome in its own right, so I tend not to go overboard when cooking it. Here I am simply grilling it with honey and mustard and serving it with another taste of my own childhood – mashed potato mixed with peas. If you prefer, you can omit the mustard and it will still be a delicious meal.

1 Bring a large saucepan of salted water to the boil and cook the potato for 15 minutes, until it is nice and tender.
2 Preheat the grill. Mix the honey and mustard together in a bowl and brush or spread half the marinade on to the steaks.
3 With 6 to 7 minutes left for the potatoes to cook, grill the steaks in a grill pan or ovenproof baking dish for 5 minutes, then turn them over, cover them with the remaining honey and mustard mix and grill for another 5 minutes.
4 Add the peas 3 minutes before the potatoes have finished cooking. Drain the potatoes and peas, return them to the saucepan on a medium heat and let some of the absorbed water steam off for a minute or two.
5 Mash the potatoes and peas and mix in the milk and butter.
6 Season the potatoes with salt and pepper, put a dollop of mash on each plate, a gammon steak on top and drizzle with any remaining cooking juices from the grill.

Serves 4

Preparation time 10 minutes

Cooking time 20 minutes

1kg potatoes, peeled and cut into small chunks

2 handfuls of frozen peas

2–3 tablespoons honey

1 teaspoon Dijon mustard

4 x 100g gammon steaks

A glug of milk

A knob of butter

Salt and freshly ground black pepper

Baked penne with courgette and home-made Italian sausage

The home-made Italian sausage mix I use in this recipe is extremely quick and easy to make and will really enhance this delicious rustic dish. You can always use mince from good-quality sausages, but I actually think it takes just as long to cut them open and squeeze out the meat as it does to mix together the few ingredients listed here. Not forgetting, of course, that squelching mince meat is always great fun for willing little hands!

Preheat your oven to 180°C/350°F/Gas Mark 4.

1 Put a large saucepan of salted water on to boil and cook the penne according to the instructions on the packet.
2 Meanwhile, make the sausage mince. You will need to grind the fennel seeds using a pestle and mortar. If you don't have a pestle and mortar, put the seeds in a plastic sandwich bag and crush them with the tip of a large rolling pin. Mix all the ingredients together in a bowl. It is worth taking a little time over this to make sure everything is evenly mixed in.
3 Heat some olive oil in a frying pan and cook the sausage meat until it is no longer pink.
4 Pour in the tomato passata, the grated courgette, season with salt and pepper and continue to cook for just a minute or two.
5 In a large baking dish, mix the cooked penne well with the sausage sauce and cover the pasta with the two grated cheeses. You want to make sure that there is a really good layer of cheese, covering much of the pasta.
6 Bake in the oven for 20 to 25 minutes, until the top is golden and bubbling.

Serves 4

Preparation time 10 minutes

Cooking time 30 minutes

450g dried penne

Olive oil

500ml tomato passata

1 courgette, grated

Salt and freshly ground black pepper

3 large handfuls of grated extra-mature Cheddar cheese

1 large handful of freshly grated Parmesan cheese

For the Italian sausage mix:
1 tablespoon fennel seeds

500g pork mince

2 teaspoons garlic powder

1 tablespoon mild paprika

Freshly ground black pepper and a good pinch of salt

Fish roasted with an easy sun-dried tomato tapenade

It is fair to say that white fish such as cod and haddock can be a little bland when cooked on their own. A simple and quick way of jazzing up these pieces of fish is to create a sauce, a paste or a crust, spread it over the fillets and simply bake them in an oven. This first version has a strong Mediterranean hint, adding flavour to a classic tapenade by using sun-dried tomatoes. The tapenade can be made up to a week in advance and stored in the fridge in an airtight container. If you have any left over, just stir it into pasta for the easiest lunchtime meal.

Both this recipe and the tarragon and lemon-crusted fish (see opposite) go very well with the crushed new potatoes from the pork escalope recipe on page 160 and simple green vegetables.

Preheat your oven to 200°C/400°F/Gas Mark 6.

1 Blend the sun-dried tomatoes, the olives, pine nuts, garlic, the capers and the optional anchovies in a food mixer or food processor. Just pulse them gently and in short bursts – you want a rough paste rather than a purée.
2 Mix in the olive oil, stopping at 4 tablespoons if the tapenade looks like it is becoming too loose and liquid. Finally, add in the herbs, the lemon juice and the freshly ground black pepper.
3 Lightly oil a baking sheet or baking tray. Pat the fish filets dry with some kitchen paper.
4 Spread some tapenade onto each fillet, pat it down a little so that it is well set, then fluff the top up a little with a fork.
5 Bake for 15 minutes, or until the fish is cooked through, and then serve immediately.

Serves 4

Preparation time 10–15 minutes

Cooking time 15 minutes

150g sun-dried tomatoes, drained from their oil

100g pitted green olives in brine, drained and very thoroughly rinsed

2 tablespoons pine nuts

2 garlic cloves

1 teaspoon capers, drained, rinsed and 'dried' on some absorbent kitchen paper

3 anchovy fillets (optional – if you happen to have a tin open, otherwise it can be a waste to just use a few fillets)

4–5 tablespoons olive oil

1 teaspoon herbes de Provence

1 tablespoon lemon juice

Freshly ground black pepper

4 x good-sized (approx 170g) cod or haddock fillets (or any other firm white fish), skin removed

Tarragon and lemon-crusted fish

This second fish crust recipe is a slightly crunchier affair. Tarragon, most often associated with chicken, is rather lovely with fish too and the zesty lemon really, really zings up its soft aniseedy flavour. With the addition of Parmesan, this is a dish bursting with flavour. Almost any firm white fish can work for this recipe – the thicker the better because this will help them stay moist in the oven.

Preheat your oven to 220°C/425°F/Gas Mark 7.

1 Melt the butter in a non-metallic bowl in the microwave for 20 seconds (or in a pan on the hob).
2 Mix together all the ingredients except the fish, then cover each fillet well with a good dollop of the mixture, pressing down slightly so it sticks well.
3 Lightly oil a baking tray, lay the fillets on it and bake for approximately 15 minutes or until the crust has turned golden and the fish is fully cooked through. Serve immediately.

Serves 4

Preparation time 10 minutes

Cooking time 15 minutes

2 tablespoons butter

50g coarse breadcrumbs

15g tarragon, chopped

Grated zest of 1 lemon

25g freshly grated Parmesan cheese

1 teaspoon Dijon or wholegrain mustard

Salt and freshly ground black pepper

4 x 175g thick white fish fillets, skin removed

Tandoori salmon with a cucumber salad

Salmon is a sturdy fish and can really cope with the fragrant flavours of the spice mix. I would describe this really lovely tandoori paste as warm rather than spicy, but if you want to give it a bit of an extra kick, just add ¼ teaspoon chilli powder to the marinade. Although the recipe list may, at first, seem a little long, it is made up of simple cupboard spices and ingredients. While you can happily serve the salmon with plain rice, I am giving it a lighter, summery touch by serving it with salad, naan bread and a minty yoghurt sauce. The marinade will of course be just as tasty on chicken.

Preheat your grill to high.

1 Mix together all the marinade ingredients and leave the salmon to marinate for anything between a few minutes at room temperature and a few hours in the fridge.
2 Mix together the yoghurt, mint sauce and cumin and leave in the fridge until the salmon is cooked.
3 Cover a baking tray with aluminium foil and grease with a little oil. Take the salmon fillets out of the marinade, shaking off any excess, and lay them on the baking tray. Grill the fillets on a high shelf just under the grill for 8 to 10 minutes, until they have started to crisp up and are just cooked through.
4 Take the salmon out from under the grill and quickly grill the naan bread, as per the instructions on the packet.
5 Serve each plate with one fillet of salmon, a handful of chopped tomato, cucumber and red onion and some naan bread – leaving the minty yoghurt in a bowl on the table for everyone to serve themselves from.

Serves 4

Preparation time 10–15 minutes (plus marinating)

Cooking time 10 minutes

4 x 175g salmon fillets, skin removed

2 large (or 4 small) naan breads

For the tandoori marinade:
1 teaspoon garam masala

1 teaspoon ground coriander

1 teaspoon ground cumin

A pinch of turmeric

A good pinch of salt

Juice of ½ lemon

3 tablespoons tomato purée

2 garlic cloves, crushed

1.5cm cube of fresh ginger, grated

150g plain yoghurt

2 tablespoons vegetable or groundnut oil

For the minty yoghurt:
150g plain yoghurt

2 teaspoons mint sauce

A small pinch of ground cumin

For the salad:
½ cucumber, roughly chopped

4 very ripe tomatoes, roughly chopped

1 red onion, halved and thinly sliced

Miso-glazed grilled fish

This is a lovely and subtle way of jazzing up a humble piece of white fish. Miso paste is available in most supermarkets and it keeps in the fridge for ages. In fact, legend has it that it is impossible for it to EVER go off, but it's probably best not to quote me on that! Using miso paste has two advantages – it gives a subtle sweet flavour to the fish and also turns a golden glazed colour when grilled. It's hard to think of a simpler and tastier way to liven up your midweek fish meals.

1 Cook the rice according to the instructions on the packet.
2 In a bowl, mix together the miso paste, the sugar, the lemon juice, the olive oil and the sesame seeds.
3 Pat the fish dry with some kitchen paper and then generously brush the top of each fillet with plenty of the miso marinade.
4 Heat up your grill. With the rice due to be ready in 7 minutes or so, cook some green vegetables to go with the fish.
5 At the same time, put the fish fillets on a baking tray or grill pan and grill them for 6 to 8 minutes (it will depend on the thickness of the fillets).
6 The fish is ready when it is cooked through and has started to take on a slightly crispy glaze. Serve immediately with the rice and vegetables.

Serves 4

Preparation time 10 minutes

Cooking time 15 minutes

250g jasmine rice

3 tablespoons white miso paste

1½ tablespoons sugar (I recommend golden caster sugar for this dish)

2 tablespoons lemon juice

A few drizzles of olive oil

A handful of sesame seeds

4 x 175g white fish fillets, skin removed

Green vegetables, to serve

Moroccan cod kebabs with minty lemon tabouleh

There is a wonderful Moroccan spice mix called *chermoula* and I have yet to find the definitive recipe for it. This means that you can mix and match quantities (and ingredients, for that matter) in the spice mix and still cook something lovely. Archie doesn't love very spicy seasoning, so I tend to leave the chilli out and just sprinkle some cayenne pepper on mine and Jo's. That said, I have seen some kids with an Olympian chilli threshold, so don't be afraid to leave it in if you know if will not offend. I am serving this with a version of a 'tabouleh' salad. You can make it in advance and chill it in the fridge or simply prepare it while the fish is cooking. Both the marinade and the salad require fresh flat-leaf parsley and mint. Buy 25g packets of each and use half for the marinade and half for the salad.

If you are using wooden skewers under the grill, you will need to soak them in water beforehand so that they don't burn.

1 In a food mixer, blender or pestle and mortar, mix all the spice mix ingredients together until they form a smooth paste. If you have none of these instruments, just chop the mint, coriander, parsley, garlic and chilli finely and mix with the other ingredients in a bowl.
2 Mix the fish into the paste. Ideally the fish should be left to marinate for an hour or so, but this is not actually essential. Thread the fish and the red peppers equally on to four skewers and heat up your oven's grill or a griddle pan.
3 Make the tabouleh. Boil a kettle, pour the bulgar wheat into a saucepan, drizzle over some olive oil and pour in enough boiling water to cover it, plus an extra 5mm on top. Cover the saucepan and leave the bulgar for the time specified on the packet to absorb the water.
4 Cook the fish kebabs either under the grill or on a griddle pan for 6 to 8 minutes, turning them regularly to ensure all sides are equally cooked.
5 Just before the fish has finished grilling, mix the herbs, tomato, the lemon juice and 4 tablespoons olive oil into the cooked bulgar wheat and season with a little salt and pepper.
6 Serve the fish and the tabouleh salad with a bowl of plain yoghurt on the side.

Serves 4

Preparation time 15–20 minutes (plus 1 hour marinating if possible)

Cooking time 10 minutes

700g chunky cod fillets, cut into large 3cm cubes

2 red peppers, cut into 3cm squares

Plain yoghurt, to serve

For the spice mix:
1 handful of mint

2 handfuls of coriander leaves

1 handful of flat-leaf parsley

3 garlic cloves

1 red chilli, deseeded (optional)

1 teaspoon ground coriander

1 teaspoon paprika

A few strands of saffron or 1 teaspoon of turmeric

Juice of ½ lemon

100ml olive oil

For the tabouleh:
200g bulgar wheat (you can use couscous too)

Olive oil

A handful of mint, chopped

A handful of flat-leaf parsley, chopped

8 cherry tomatoes, quartered

Juice of 1 lemon

Grilled breaded pork escalopes with crushed new potatoes

These delicious escalopes are brilliant for creative play with a little helper in the kitchen because preparing them involves banging, dipping, rolling and even painting with butter! They cook very quickly under the grill and come up beautifully crunchy and golden. Putting them under the grill also means that you can cook all the mini escalopes in one batch, which you wouldn't be able to do in a frying pan.

1 Bring a large saucepan of salted water to the boil and cook the new potatoes for 15 to 20 minutes until they are soft.

2 Meanwhile, slice the tenderloin into 5mm slices. You will also need to flatten them a little more using a rolling pin. Take two sheets of greaseproof paper, put a slice of pork between the sheets and bang with the rolling pin so it becomes a little thinner. Repeat for all the slices.

3 Mix the breadcrumbs in a bowl with the rosemary and garlic powder.

4 Season the flour with a small pinch of salt and some ground pepper and dip a slice of pork into it, giving it a good dusting and shaking off any excess. Dip the slice immediately in the egg and then roll it in the breadcrumb mix to get a good covering. Repeat for all the other pieces of pork.

5 Melt the butter in a non-metallic bowl in the microwave (or in a pan on the hob). Using a pastry brush, 'paint' the escalopes on both sides with the butter, giving each one a good coating.

6 Heat up your grill and, with 5 minutes of cooking time left for the potatoes, grill the escalopes for 3 minutes on both sides, or until they are lovely and golden.

7 Drain the potatoes and simply 'pop' each one open using the underside of a fork. You don't need to mash or crush them. Pour in a really good glug of olive oil, season with salt and pepper and just stir the potatoes with a wooden spoon.

8 Serve the escalopes and the potatoes immediately, with a little green salad or simple green vegetables.

Serves 4

Preparation time 20 minutes

Cooking time 20 minutes

1kg new potatoes

1 pork tenderloin fillet (approx 450–500g), trimmed of fat

100g breadcrumbs

1½ teaspoons dried rosemary

½ teaspoon garlic powder

A saucer of plain flour

Salt and freshly ground black pepper

2 eggs, beaten

50g butter

Lots of olive oil

Grilled lemon grass and coconut chicken

I sometimes forget how tasty and easy grilled chicken can be, especially when the meat is tenderised by a marinade such as this simple coconut and lemon grass mix. Served with plain jasmine rice and steamed greens, this is a lovely, simple midweek meal.

1 In a bowl or, preferably, a blender or food mixer, blend the garlic, lemon grass, the sugar, lime juice, soy sauce, fish sauce, turmeric (if using) and 5 tablespoons of the coconut milk together.
2 Make three diagonal cuts across the skin of each chicken breast and rub the marinade all over them. Ideally you would leave the chicken and the marinade in the fridge for at least 30 minutes, but if you simply don't have time, you can grill them immediately.
3 Heat up your grill. While it is heating up, place the rice in a saucepan, pour in the remainder of the coconut milk and add enough water to just cover the rice. Bring to the boil and simmer for 5 minutes, then take the rice off the heat, cover tightly with a lid and simply leave the saucepan for 15 minutes while you cook the chicken.
4 Put the chicken breasts in a grill pan and grill for 15 minutes, turning and basting occasionally with a spoon.
5 Cook your green vegetables while the chicken is grilling.
6 Once the chicken is cooked, leave it to rest in the pan for a few minutes while you fluff up the rice with a fork, then serve together with your vegetables and wedges of lime.

Serves 4

Preparation time 10 minutes

Cooking time 20 minutes

2 garlic cloves, crushed

1 stalk of lemon grass (hard outer layer removed), chopped finely

2 tablespoons brown sugar

Juice of 1 lime

Dash of light soy sauce

A few drops of Thai fish sauce

A pinch of turmeric (optional)

400g tin coconut milk

4 chicken breasts, skin on

300g jasmine rice

1 lime, cut into wedges

Tartiflette

When I lived in France, my nickname there was Monsieur Catastrophe. It was a fitting epithet. If there was a door to bang into, a pavement to fall over, an expensive piece of china to drop, you could always count on me. This appetite for clumsiness is probably one of the reasons I have never braved a ski slope. With tartiflette being the traditional dish of the Savoie region and an après-ski classic, this recipe may be as near to the slopes as I will get for the foreseeable future. One of my absolute favourite dishes, this tartiflette is indulgent comfort food at its finest.

Preheat your oven to 200°C/400°F/Gas Mark 6.

1 Bring a large pan of water to the boil and cook the potato slices for 8 to 10 minutes until they are just starting to get cooked through. You don't want to overcook them or they will fall apart. Drain them once cooked.

2 While the potatoes are cooking, heat some olive oil (although not too much) in a pan on a medium heat and cook the onion and garlic until they are soft. Add the pancetta and cook for a further couple of minutes. If you have a bottle of white wine to hand, pour in a splash of it and let it reduce down for a few minutes. Season with salt and pepper, going gently with the salt, though, as the bacon is already salty enough.

3 Take a good-sized baking dish, grease it with a little butter and put one layer of the potatoes on the base. Spoon on some of the bacon and onion mixture, add another layer of potatoes, and then some more bacon and onion. Carry on doing this until you have used up all the ingredients, making sure that the top layer is potato.

4 Scrape the crust of the Reblochon a little with a knife to remove the outer coating, then cut the cheese in half horizontally, giving you a top half and a bottom half. Put the two discs, crust facing upwards, on to the top layer of potatoes and bake for about 30 minutes, keeping an eye on the dish so that the cheese doesn't burn.

5 Serve immediately with nothing more than a light green salad.

Serves 4

Preparation time 10 minutes

Cooking time 40 minutes

1kg potatoes, peeled and thickly sliced

Olive oil

1 large onion, cut in half and sliced very thinly

1 garlic clove, chopped

A couple of good handfuls of diced pancetta or lardons

A splash of white wine (optional)

Salt and freshly ground black pepper

1 whole Reblochon cheese

Creamy wild mushroom and Parma ham pasta bake

You may decide you don't need to actually bake this pasta. It is certainly very tasty served straight out of the pan but I love the old-fashioned, slightly dry crispiness of the pasta when it's cooked a little in the oven. And of course, baking it has the double advantage of meaning it can be prepared well in advance. Wild mushrooms are not cheap, but this recipe only calls for one 20g pack. It's amazing how much flavour so few mushrooms can give a dish. Supermarkets now stock all manner of fresh mushrooms and any mix of them will work well. Feel free to omit the ham if you want to serve this as a vegetarian dish or reduce the cost – the finished product will not suffer for it.

Preheat your oven to 180°C/350°F/Gas Mark 4.

1 Cover the dried mushrooms in boiling water and soak them for 10 minutes.
2 Put a large saucepan of salted water on to boil and cook your pasta according to the instructions on the packet. Drain and cool when it's cooked.
3 Meanwhile, in a frying pan on a medium heat, melt the butter and cook the shallot for 4 minutes. Add the fresh mushrooms and garlic and continue to cook for a few minutes.
4 Drain the dried mushrooms, saving the liquid, chop them up and add them to the pan.
5 When the mushrooms look well cooked, add the ham and pour in the wine and a few tablespoons of the liquid you soaked the mushrooms in (if it looks 'gritty', strain it through a sieve first).
6 Simmer for a few minutes and let the liquid reduce by a third and then pour in the crème fraîche.
7 Add the basil, season the sauce, and simmer gently for a further couple of minutes.
8 Mix the sauce, the pasta and half the Parmesan in a baking dish and sprinkle the remaining Parmesan over the top.
9 Bake in the oven for about 10 minutes, until the top has crisped up and gone golden.

Serves 4

Preparation time
10–15 minutes

Cooking time 35 minutes

20g dried porcini mushrooms

450g dried rigatoni or penne

2 tablespoons butter

2 shallots, chopped

450g mixed fresh mushrooms, such as chestnut and shiitake, sliced

2 garlic cloves, crushed

100g Parma ham or similar, cut into strips

150ml white wine

300ml half-fat crème fraîche

A handful of basil leaves, chopped

Salt and freshly ground black pepper

150g freshly grated Parmesan cheese

9
Puds, Treats and Sweets

Possibly the messiest chapter of this book and undoubtedly the most indulgent, but is there any greater pleasure in the kitchen than making sweet treats with children and then eating them together? None of these recipes require any great precision so, even if ingredients end up all over the kitchen (as they usually do when Archie and I bake together), the results will still be delicious every time.

Individual decaf tiramisu glasses

I have cheated on some things with this devilish version of a tiramisu, but not on others. Ideally you should use strong espresso coffee to dip the sponge finger biscuits in, but the thought of such a strong hit of caffeine in a little body brings up images of my toddler staying awake for 36 hours! Of course, the traditional tiramisu also has Marsala or brandy in it, and I have kept alcohol out of these too. In return for not risking turning Archie into a half-drunk whirling dervish, I haven't skimped on any of the other ingredients. I have often seen tiramisu lightened by omitting the mascarpone cheese or the cream, but I will not be doing that here. Even without the alcohol and the caffeine hit, these tiramisus are still indulgent and unctuous – just as they should be. Better still, they are an easy joy to put together.

‘

1 Make your coffee, stir in 1 tablespoon of the sugar and leave it to cool to room temperature.
2 Mix together the mascarpone with one third (60ml) of the coffee, the vanilla extract, the cream and the remaining tablespoon of sugar. Taste the mixture. If you feel it still needs a little sweetening, add some extra sugar.
3 Dunk four biscuits at a time in the remaining coffee, making sure each one absorbs a good amount of liquid, and stand the four biscuits up in one of the glasses. Don't worry if they break or squash a little. Repeat for the other three glasses.
4 Spoon equal amounts of the cream mix into each of the four glasses and put them in the fridge for a minimum of 30 minutes. It will not do them any harm if they are in the fridge for a few hours or even overnight.
5 When you are ready to serve, take them out of the fridge, cover them with a thick layer of grated chocolate and finish off with a dusting of cocoa powder.

Serves 4

Preparation time 15–20 minutes (plus at least 30 minutes' setting)

You will need four good-sized glasses

A cup of decaffeinated coffee (made up from 175ml boiling water and 5 teaspoons instant decaffeinated coffee powder)

2 tablespoons caster sugar

250g mascarpone

A little drop of vanilla extract

100ml single cream

16 sponge finger biscuits

50g dark chocolate, grated

Cocoa powder, for dusting

Hot citrus pudding (with its own citrus sauce)

Beware of first appearances. This dessert is so unassuming when taken out of the oven and yet it is hiding its own brilliant surprise. As you would expect, the mixture forms a lovely soft pudding when baked. But somehow all the citrus juices also drop to the base of the dish, forming a curdy, citrusy sauce. All so simple and yet all so very tasty!

Stages 1 to 4 can be done more quickly in a food mixer.

Preheat the oven to 180°C/350°F/Gas Mark 4.

1 Place the butter and sugar in a bowl and beat with a wooden spoon until it starts to go pale in colour.
2 Separate the yolks and the egg whites. The easiest way to do this is to crack the eggs into your cupped hand and let the egg whites trickle through your fingers into a bowl while your palm keeps the yolk. Whisk the egg yolks into the butter and sugar.
3 Mix in the grated lemon, orange and lime zests, followed by the juices.
4 Fold the flour into the mix and finally add the milk.
5 In a clean bowl with a clean whisk, whisk the egg whites. You need them to reach the stage where stiff peaks are formed when you pull the whisk out of the bowl.
6 Take a metal spoon, add the whisked egg whites into the citrus mix and fold them in lightly, using a figure-of-eight movement. You don't want to stir here or else the egg whites will lose all their air.
7 Pour the mix into the baking dish and cook for 40 minutes, or until the pudding has risen and the top is golden and firm to the touch.
8 Leave to cool for a few minutes and serve immediately.

Serves 6

Preparation time 15–20 minutes

Cooking time 40 minutes

You will need a 2 inch (5cm) deep baking dish

75g softened butter

175g caster sugar

3 eggs

Grated zest and juice of 1 lemon

Grated zest and juice of 1 orange

Grated zest and juice of 2 limes

75g self-raising flour

200ml milk (semi-skimmed or full-fat)

Creamy berry shortbreads

Anyone who loves cooking in the kitchen with kids loves baking biscuits, so I had to have at least one biscuit recipe in this book. This recipe takes a classic shortbread and elevates it to finger-licking status with the addition of whipped cream and red fruits.

Preheat the oven to 180°C/350°F/Gas Mark 4.

1 Mix together the plain flour, the cornflour and the icing sugar, then throw in the butter and rub all the ingredients together, using the tips of your fingers, until the mixture resembles fine crumbs.
2 Add in the egg yolk and mix all the ingredients together to get a light dough, which should not be handled too much. Be gentle with it and the biscuits will be much softer.
3 If you have 15 minutes spare, leave the pastry to chill in some clingfilm in the fridge. If not, just roll the dough out thinly (approximately 5mm) on a well-floured surface and use a round biscuit cutter or bowl to cut out discs. A 10cm cutter should give you at least eight circles. Make sure you use all the dough by gathering up the trimmings and rolling out gently again.
4 Carefully lift the discs off the worktop using a knife or spatula and put them on a baking tray lined with greaseproof paper. If the dough had a chance to chill, the discs will be nice and firm. If you didn't have a chance to chill it, you will simply need to handle the discs with care so they don't lose their shape.
5 Bake for approximately 12 minutes or until the biscuits start to go a little golden.
6 While the biscuits are baking, whisk the whipping cream and a drop of vanilla extract until light and fluffy. Chill the cream until you are ready to use it.
7 When cooked, take the biscuits out of the oven and leave them to cool.
8 Just before serving, place a layer of berries on four biscuits. Spread some whipped cream on each and top with another biscuit to form 'sandwiches'. Dust the top biscuits with a little extra icing sugar using a sieve.

Makes 4 shortcake and raspberry 'sandwiches'

Preparation time 15 minutes (plus 15 minutes chilling if possible)

Cooking time 12 minutes

190g plain flour

60g cornflour

60g icing sugar

150g softened butter, diced

1 egg yolk

200ml whipping cream

A few drops of vanilla extract

250g any red berries

Raspberry sponge crumble squares

We love making sponges together (as you will have seen on the videos on the blog, the mix usually ends up anywhere other than in the baking tin and yet still makes a great cake!) and we love making the mix for crumbles. This dessert brings together the best of both, adding a crumble topping to a lovely raspberry sponge. The potential for extreme mess cannot be overstated, but the resulting crumble squares make it all more than worthwhile!

Preheat your oven to 180°C/350°F/Gas Mark 4.

1 Make the crumble mix. Rub the butter into the flour with your fingertips, then mix in the sugar. You can also do this with a quick blitz in a food processor.
2 For the sponge, cream together the butter and sugar in a food processor or with a bowl and wooden spoon until the mix is light and a little fluffy.
3 Mix in the eggs, one by one, and then mix in the flour and the lemon and orange zest
4 Finally, mix in the raspberries.
5 Grease a rectangular baking tin and line the base with greaseproof paper.
6 Pour in the cake mix and then gently sprinkle the crumble mix over the top. You don't want it to mix into the cake mix. Push down gently on the crumble mix so it is well set (of course, Archie put his hands right through the mix when invited to do this!)
7 Bake for around 50 minutes. Keep an eye on the cake – it is ready when the sponge has risen and the crumble topping is golden.
8 Leave the cake to cool down, then cut it into squares. They can be frozen or will keep for a good few days in an airtight container.

Makes about 25 squares

Preparation time 15–20 minutes

Cooking time 50–55 minutes

For the crumble topping:

80g butter, chopped up

130g plain flour

50g demerara sugar

For the sponge:

175g softened butter

175g caster sugar

3 eggs

175g self-raising flour

Finely grated zest of 1 lemon

Finely grated zest of 1 orange

150g raspberries

Microwave chocolate steamed pudding (with its own chocolate sauce)

Yes, a cake, in the microwave! With its own delicious sauce trapped underneath, this really is my kind of dessert. It's oozy, very rich – and it's a complete cheat. Normally you'd cook puddings like this in baking trays in the oven, steamed in a bath of hot water. Too 'cheffy' for this book, without a doubt. This pudding takes a matter of minutes to put together, then it's a simple ping and ding operation. Ping the microwave, wait 7 to 8 minutes, ding and it is cooked. Don't ask how it all magically comes together, I honestly am not sure!

1 In a wide, deep, flat-bottomed (non-metallic) bowl, melt the butter in the microwave for 90 seconds.
2 Sift in the flour, add the caster sugar, half the cocoa powder, the milk and the vanilla extract and stir it all together well until you get a smooth cake mix.
3 Mix the soft brown sugar and the remaining cocoa powder together and sprinkle it over the top of the cake mix.
4 Pour over 275ml boiling water, but do not mix it in.
5 Put the bowl on a plate (the sauce may drip over the edge of the bowl) in the microwave and cook on full power for 7 minutes. The cake should be spongy on the top and springy when you press on it. If it is still a little soggy, cook for a further minute.
6 Take it out of the microwave, leave to rest for a few minutes, then serve immediately as the pudding is not great once it has cooled down. The sauce itself is quite liquid, so it needs to be spooned over the sponge in each bowl, not drizzled to the side.

Serves 4 big mouths,
6 smaller ones

Preparation time 10 minutes

Cooking time 10 minutes

55g butter

200g self-raising flour

170g caster sugar

55g good-quality cocoa powder

180ml milk

A few good drops of vanilla extract

110g soft brown sugar

Baked cinnamon apples

My mum is a great cook and, in many ways, this whole book comes from what I have learned from her. It does feel a little like I am damning her with faint praise if I am putting my take on this extremely simple retro childhood favourite in the book as a tribute to her, but simple is good and she used to make this pudding almost more often than we had hot dinners. The tradition has carried on today and her grandson loves her baked apples as much as her son does. I have added some thick slices of brioche, which act as a base and mop up all the lovely sweet butter.

Preheat your oven to 160°C/325°F/Gas Mark 3.

1   If any of the apples do not sit flat, cut a thin slice off their base.
2   Mix together the raisins, sugar and butter.
3   With a sharp knife, make one light cut all round each apple, just above the centre.
4   If you are using the brioche, trim the slices so they are a similar size to the apples. Lightly grease a baking dish with butter, lay the four slices of brioche in the dish and place each apple on a slice. Fill the apples with the sugar and butter mix, letting it overflow slightly over the top.
5   Sprinkle the apples fairly generously with ground cinnamon, lightly cover the dish with aluminium foil and bake for 40 minutes, then remove the foil and bake for a further 15 to 20 minutes, or until the apples are really soft and starting to brown.
6   Serve the apples immediately, with a dollop of crème fraîche or vanilla ice cream.

Serves 4

Preparation time 5 minutes

Cooking time 1 hour

4 cooking apples, cored

A handful of raisins

3 tablespoons soft brown sugar

3 tablespoons butter

4 thick slices of slightly stale brioche (optional)

Ground cinnamon

Crème fraîche or vanilla ice cream, to serve

Muddy flourless chocolate cake

This is without any doubt the best chocolate cake I have ever made. It is just devilishly good – rich, moist, muddy, chocolaty – and was a huge hit on the blog when we made it for Valentine's Day. It also has the added bonus of being suitable for anyone with a wheat and gluten allergy as the ground almonds completely remove the need for flour. The cake gets the full My Daddy Cooks treatment as I strip many of the traditional stages out of the preparation. For example, instead of creaming together the butter and sugar – as most classic versions of this cake require – I just throw them in the hot chocolate and melt them. And having tried both the intricate version and my own pared down version, I would even say that this version is better! Plus you'll have the extra pleasure of serving up a posh-looking cake in the full knowledge that it was child's play to make it.

Preheat your oven to 180°C/350°F/Gas Mark 4.

1 Prepare the cake tin by lining the base with greaseproof paper and greasing the sides with butter.
2 Separate the yolks and the egg whites. The easiest way to do this is to crack the eggs into your cupped hand and let the egg whites trickle through your fingers into a bowl while your palm keeps the yolk.
3 Sit a bowl on a saucepan of barely simmering water. The bowl should not be touching the water. Put the chocolate in the bowl and let it melt.
4 When the chocolate has melted, throw in the butter and sugar and mix well until everything is fully liquid.
5 Take the bowl off the pan and mix in the almonds and then the egg yolks, one at a time. Leave that mixture to cool a little to room temperature.
6 While the chocolate mix is cooling, add a small pinch of salt to the egg whites (it helps the whites to whisk into stiff peaks), then beat the egg whites using an electric whisk, hand whisk or food mixer with the whisk attachment until firm and fluffy. You know the whites are ready if you dip a whisk into them, pull it out and it leaves a stiff peak in the mix.

This recipe will make at least 10 slices. The cake tastes better even after a night in the fridge, so there is no need to worry about making too much.

Preparation time 15–20 minutes

Cooking time 40 minutes

You will need an 8 inch (20cm) round cake tin

6 eggs

200g good-quality dark chocolate (at least 60% cocoa solids – 70% works best)

180g unsalted butter

180g caster sugar

180g ground almonds

A pinch of salt

Icing sugar, to dust the cake

7 Mix a couple of spoonfuls of the whisked egg whites into the chocolate mix, just to loosen it up. Then, using a metal spoon, add the rest of the whites and fold them in. This basically means don't stir them heavily. Fold them in using a figure-of-eight movement with the spoon. This preserves the air in the mix.

8 Pour the cake mix into your prepared cake tin and bake it in the middle of your oven for about 40 minutes. It is better to slightly undercook this cake than overcook it. It will carry on cooking anyway while it cools down.

9 Take the cake out of the oven, leave it to cool a little in its tin, then turn it out to cool on a rack (it's not a big deal if it cools on a plate instead).

10 Put some icing sugar in a sieve and gently dust the top of the cake. Serve warm, cold or even the next day...

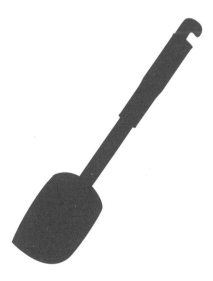

Microwave lemon treacle pudding

And here is my second microwave cake. It's also my second homage to my favourite dinner lady and my favourite school treat – treacle pudding. I used to love the surprise of peeking over the top of the serving counter and seeing large rectangular dishes of sponge with dripping golden syrup on top. I also used to have an unfounded aversion to custard, so always ate mine simply on its own. This version adds some lemon tanginess and it's great to use the microwave for this type of sponge, not least because it cuts the cooking time by a couple of hours. If you don't have a microwave, simply put the pudding dish in a pan, cover it securely, pour in enough water to come up to halfway up the sides of the pudding, and bring to the boil and simmer for 1½ hours.

You will need a 1¾ pint (1 litre) pudding basin.

1 Grease your non-metallic pudding basin with a knob of butter.
2 In a small bowl, mix together the breadcrumbs, the golden syrup and the lemon juice, then pour the mixture into the pudding basin.
3 Beat the butter together with the lemon zest and sugar until it goes light and fluffy, then slowly add the eggs. Stir in the flour and then add the milk. You can of course skip all of this and just bung everything in a food mixer!
4 Pour this mix into the pudding basin and cover (not too tightly) with clingfilm.
5 Cook on full power in the microwave. As all microwaves are notoriously different from each other, check the pudding after 5 minutes by inserting a skewer. If the pudding is cooked, the skewer will come out dry. If it is still a little sticky, cook for an extra 30 seconds and check again.
6 Once the pudding is cooked, leave it to rest for 3 minutes (still covered) and then turn it out on to a plate.
7 Eat it immediately with custard or clotted cream.

Serves 4

Preparation time 10 minutes

Cooking time 5 minutes

1 thick slice of white bread, crusts removed, crumbled

3 tablespoons golden syrup

Zest of 1 lemon, plus 1 tablespoon juice

140g softened unsalted butter

140g caster sugar

2 large eggs, beaten

140g self-raising flour

3 tablespoons milk

Custard or clotted cream, to serve

No-bake chocolate tiffin cake

When it came to deciding which of the few recipes I should take from the blog and include in the book, this was at the very top of the list. This tiffin cake involves no baking and by the time you have made it every other day for a week, you will be preparing it in under 5 minutes. It is actually hard to describe quite how delicious it is. All I can say is you will not find a quicker route to chocolate heaven. Quite a few people mentioned on the blog that it would not be ruined by adding some small marshmallows – and I would have to agree! Be sure to use a high-quality cocoa powder if you can, it really does make a difference.

1 Pour the golden syrup into a non-metallic bowl with the butter and melt in the microwave on full power for about 1½ to 2 minutes (you can also do this in a pan on the hob).

2 While the butter and syrup are melting, put the biscuits in a plastic bag, seal it and bash them up. You don't want them to crumble to a powder. The chunky bits are the best bits in the tiffin.

3 Add the cocoa, the raisins and then the biscuit to the melted butter and golden syrup. Pour the mix into a tin and spread it evenly, flattening it down as you go.

4 Melt the chocolate in the microwave for 2 to 3 minutes (it will depend on the power of your microwave) or melt it in a bowl sitting on (but not touching) a saucepan of barely simmering water. Spread the melted chocolate evenly over the biscuit base and then simply put the dish in the fridge.

5 The cake will be set and ready to eat within 1 hour. It keeps for several days in the fridge in an airtight container, but will likely be eaten well before!

Preparation time 10 minutes maximum (plus 1 hour in the fridge)

4 tablespoons golden syrup

125g butter

250g digestive biscuits

3 heaped tablespoons good-quality cocoa powder

75g raisins

250g plain/dark chocolate

Portuguese rice pudding

We have a truly lovely Portuguese friend called Carolina Almas who is one of the best hosts you could ever hope to meet. She introduced me to *arroz doce*, which is a Portuguese version of rice pudding. It is traditionally served at major celebrations and Christmas and people take great pride in turning the cinnamon topping into a work of art. The easiest way of doing something pretty with children is to use a paper doily as a stencil. Alternatively, Archie feels that the throw-it-all-on technique is more fun and, apparently, equally aesthetic.

1 Heat the milk in a large saucepan. When it starts to bubble, melt in the butter, then add the rice, sugar, lemon peel and the cinnamon stick.
2 Simmer for 20 minutes, until the rice is cooked and all the liquid has been absorbed.
3 Mix in the egg yolks and a pinch of salt and continue to stir for a few minutes on a very low heat.
4 Although this rice pudding can be served cold, I prefer it served warm. Spoon it either into one large serving bowl or four small ones and decorate it however you want to with the ground cinnamon.

Serves 4

Preparation time 5 minutes

Cooking time 25 minutes

750ml milk

1 tablespoon butter

250g long-grain rice

250g sugar

2 strips of lemon peel

1 cinnamon stick

3 egg yolks

Pinch of salt

Lots of ground cinnamon, to decorate

The easiest mini fudges

It's great when three basic ingredients, which you would most likely have sitting in your cupboards, come together to make an easy treat like this. This fudge recipe is based on a traditional Brazilian sweet called *brigadeiro*, which takes pride of place at all kids' parties. The fudges are fun to make (it's like doing play dough in the kitchen) and you can roll them in whatever takes your fancy.

1 Heat up the milk, the butter and the cocoa powder on a medium heat in a saucepan.
2 Keep stirring. And keep stirring more. In fact, don't stop stirring!
3 The mixture will start to thicken. Keep stirring. After 8 to 10 minutes, it will start to lift off from the bottom of the pan. This is a good sign and means your fudge is nearly ready. Keep stirring for another minute or so, then take the pan off the heat.
4 Lightly grease a bowl with some vegetable oil, put the fudge in it and leave it to cool down.
5 Grease your hands with a little oil or butter before forming the fudge into little balls by rolling small chunks of it in the palms of your hands.
6 Roll the balls well in any topping you fancy and leave them to set in small paper fairy cake cups or on a plate.

Makes about 20 little balls

They require no preparation time, except however long it takes you to roll them into shape

Cooking time 10 minutes

400g tin condensed milk

1 tablespoon butter

3 tablespoons cocoa powder

Coconut flakes/sprinkles/ hundreds and thousands, to roll the balls in

Peanut butter and chocolate brownies

When I first sat down to put together this book, I knew it would have to have a brownies recipe in it. After all, who doesn't LOVE a good brownie. But then I realised that there are already lots of brownies recipes out there, many of which I have already tried, tested, eaten and loved. So, just to be a little different, here are some wonderful peanut butter brownies. They still have their fair share of chocolate in them, but the added peanut butter gives them a gooey deliciousness, which Archie absolutely devours whenever we make them. I am giving you two options here: the rich version of just the brownie, and the double-indulgent-rich version with an easy chocolate ganache topping!

Preheat your oven to 180°C/350°F/Gas Mark 4.

1 Beat the butter and sugar together in a bowl or in a food mixer until they are light and fluffy, then add the peanut butter and continue to mix until it is really well incorporated.
2 Mix in the eggs, followed by the vanilla extract and the sifted flour and baking powder.
3 Stir in the chocolate chips (without breaking them up).
4 Grease the tin with butter and then a dusting of plain flour. Pour the mix in and bake for 40 to 45 minutes. The brownies are ready when they are golden on top and a toothpick inserted in the middle comes out with some crumbs still on it.
5 Leave the brownies to cool, then cut them into squares.

NOTE: For the optional chocolate ganache topping, bring 120ml double cream and 1 tablespoon butter gently to the boil and add in 200g dark chocolate chips (or dark chocolate, crushed into small pieces). Carry on whisking gently, until all the chocolate is melted and the mix is smooth and silky. Pour on to the cooled-down brownies and leave to set for 30 minutes or so before cutting them up.

This makes approx 16 brownies, depending on how you cut them up

Preparation time 15–20 minutes

Cooking time 45 minutes

You will need an 8 inch (20cm) square tin

200g butter

200g soft brown sugar

8 heaped tablespoons smooth peanut butter (I prefer to use a peanut butter with no added sugar)

3 eggs

2 teaspoons vanilla extract

250g plain flour

½ teaspoon baking powder

125g dark chocolate chips

Chocolate marble cake

And here is one final dessert from my childhood. This chocolate marble cake adds swirls of chocolaty joy to a classic pound cake recipe. All the fun lies in splodging in the alternate spoons of plain and chocolate cake mixture, then swirling them together to make the pretty patterns. Lovely, simple, fun family baking.

Preheat your oven to 180°C/350°F/Gas Mark 4.

1 Grease the cake tin and line the bottom with greaseproof paper.
2 Melt the chocolate in a non-metallic bowl in the microwave for 90 seconds, or until smooth. Alternatively, melt it in a bowl sitting over (but not touching) barely simmering water.
3 Beat together the butter and sugar until light and fluffy. Add the eggs one by one, then mix in the flour. Finally add the milk and vanilla extract. You can of course just blitz the whole lot together in a food mixer if you have one.
4 Divide the cake mixture into two bowls. Fold the melted chocolate into one of the bowls.
5 Using two spoons, drop the plain and chocolate cake mixes alternately into the cake tin, making sure the base is well covered.
6 Tap the cake tin against the work surface to remove any air bubbles and use a flat knife to smooth the top.
7 Using a knife or skewer, swirl through the cake mixture in whatever patterns take you or your little helper's fancy.
8 Bake for approximately 50 minutes. When an inserted skewer comes out clean, you know it is ready. Leave to cool for 5 minutes, then turn it out onto a wire rack so it can cool completely.

Preparation time 15 minutes

Cooking time 55 minutes

You will need an 8 inch (20cm) cake tin

80g plain chocolate

225g softened butter

225g caster sugar

4 eggs

225g self-raising flour

4 tablespoons milk

1½ teaspoons vanilla extract

Frozen Eton mess ice cream

This is not an ice cream in the most traditional sense because it does not require an ice-cream maker to prepare it. In fact, it requires barely any effort at all to prepare it! It's a ridiculously easy, frozen version of Eton mess, perfect for warm summer afternoons – and even dark, depressing winter evenings too. The lemon really makes all the difference here, turning the cream deliciously tangy and zesty. Although I use blackberries, raspberries would work equally well too.

1 Stir together lemon juice, the lemon zest, salt and the caster sugar until the sugar dissolves. Slowly pour in the double cream until everything is well mixed together.

2 Pour the mix into a loaf tin or a plastic container and put it in the freezer.

3 When the cream has started to freeze a little (after 90 minutes or so), take the tin out of the freezer and give it a really good stir with a fork to remove any crystals that may have formed.

4 Mix in the meringue pieces and the blackberries. The meringue will try to float up to the surface, which is unavoidable. Pop a few of the pieces down though so the big pieces are not sticking out too much. Cover the tin with clingfilm and put back in the freezer for at least 8 hours or overnight. If you do happen to be around a couple of hours after putting the tin back in the freezer, you can always give the mix another stir, but it is by no means a necessity.

5 Take the tin out of the freezer at least 20 minutes before you intend to serve as it will need time to soften. You can either serve it in scoops or turn it out onto a plate and serve in slices. If you are having difficulty turning the ice cream out of the tin, you can simply trickle some warm water over the tin and it will quickly loosen.

Serves 4 and many more (you can simply put it back in the freezer when you have finished slicing it)

Preparation time 10–15 minutes (plus at least 8 hours freezing)

Juice of 3 lemons

Grated zest of 1 lemon

A small pinch of salt

200g caster sugar

500ml double cream

2 shop-bought meringue nests, crushed into chunks

150g blackberries, roughly chopped

Plum clafoutis

This is my kind of dessert. Elaborate sounding name, unbelievably easy to make, absolutely delicious. Clafoutis originate from Normandy and are basically fruits baked in a pancake-type batter. The most traditional version uses cherries, but I find it very fiddly to eat while picking the stones out. This clafoutis uses plums, but you can use any similar stone fruits. Some people prefer to use more sugar, but I quite like letting a little bit of tartness come through from the plums. You can always sprinkle with a little extra sugar later if it is not sweet enough for your tastes.

Preheat your oven to 180°C/350°F/Gas Mark 4.

1 Grease the pie or baking dish with butter.
2 In a mixing bowl, whisk together the eggs and sugar, then add the flour and whisk again.
3 Whisk in the milk and vanilla extract until you get a really smooth batter.
4 Lay the plums out in the dish and pour over the batter so that it is just reaching the tops of the plums.
5 Bake for 30 to 40 minutes. The clafoutis is cooked when it has risen, looks golden on the top and has set in the middle. Do not take it out of the oven while it is cooking or else it will collapse.
6 When it comes out of the oven, it looks slightly unappealing. Leave it to cool a little and sink back down.
7 Put some icing sugar in a sieve and dust the clafoutis.
8 Serve it from the dish, either warm or at a good room temperature.

Serves 4–6 people

Preparation time 10 minutes

Cooking time 30–40 minutes

You will need an 8 inch (20cm) round pie dish or baking dish

3 large eggs

60g caster sugar

60g plain flour

300ml milk

½ teaspoon vanilla extract

5 or 6 ripe plums, pitted and cut in half

Icing sugar, for dusting

The number of plums you require depends on how big your dish is and how big the plums are. Don't by any means overpack the dish though as the plums let out a lot of juice and the clafoutis can become soggy

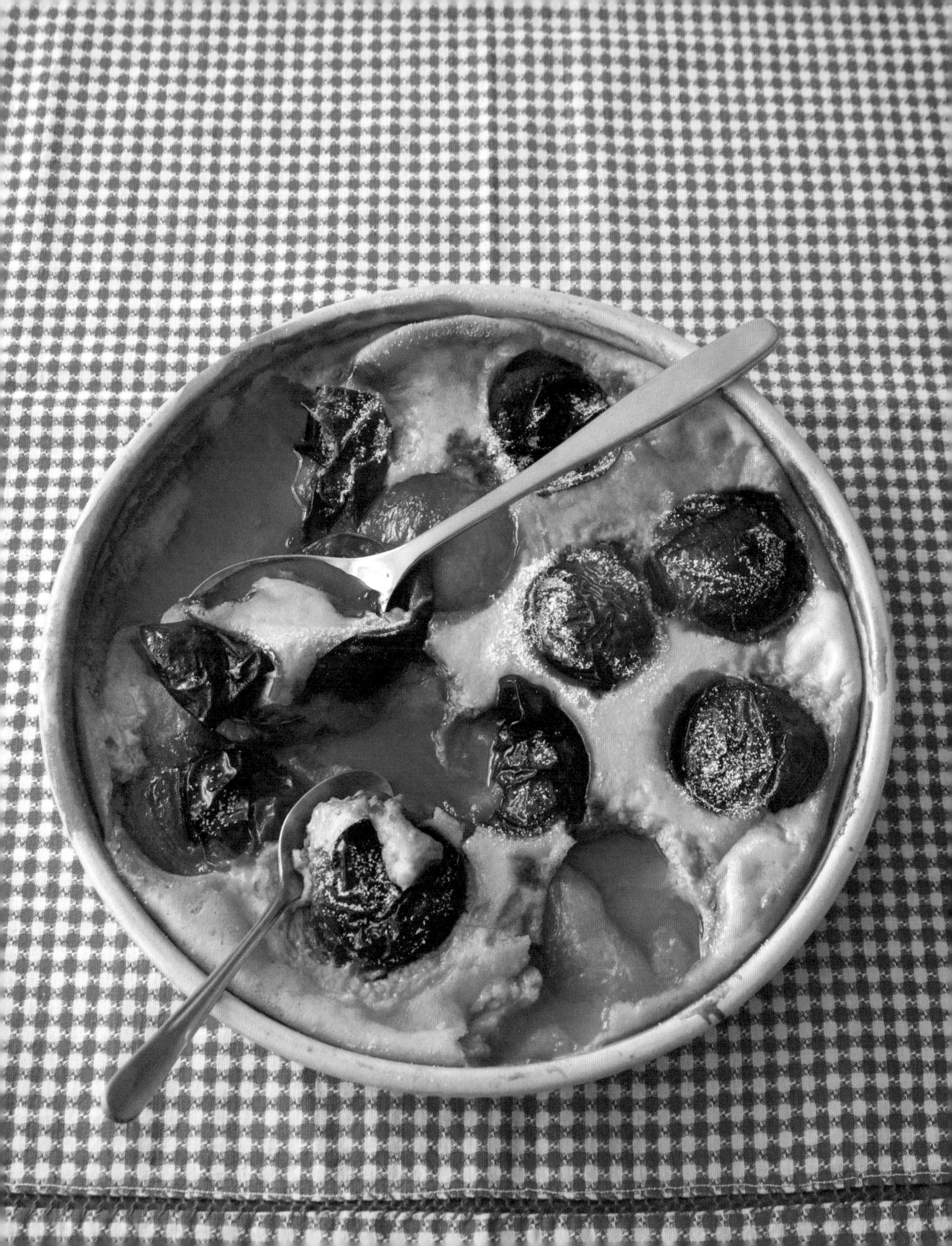

Index

Page references in **bold** indicate photographs

I firstly want to thank everyone who follows my blog. Without you there would simply be no My Daddy Cooks and I am hugely grateful to you for your support.

This book would never have happened without the expertise and support of my brilliant agent, Clare Hulton, to whom I owe a huge debt of gratitude. My lovely editor, Nicky Ross and her equally lovely assistant editor, Sarah Hammond, have guided me through the process of writing this book with incredible skill, patience and good humour. Bobby Birchall, Mark Read, Camilla Dowse and Susan Spratt worked tirelessly on the design and production of this book. Kay Halsey brilliantly edited the text of my manuscript. Véronique Leplat, her assistant Jo Castle and make-up artist Emma Coleman made the photo shoots for me and Archie effortless, fun and enjoyable. Thank you also to food stylist Katie Giovanni.

A big thank you to Emma Knight, my dynamic publicist at Hodder & Stoughton, and all the sales, marketing and rights teams, for all their invaluable hard work on this book too.

I'm incredibly grateful also to everyone who kindly offered to test and taste all the recipes in this book: Alison Chayka, Anna Moore, Becca Chapman, Chacasta and Dave Pritlove, Claire Slim, Claire Shea, Dawn McGovern, Hannah Jewell, Jan Minihane, Jen Slater, Jo Gatford, Jodi de Havilland, Karin Joyce, Katherine Jehan, Katherine Miller, Kelly and Karin Moorhouse, Lisa Fotheringham, Luschka van Onselen, Lynette Widowson, Maggy Woodley, Michelle Davies, Natasha Vessey, Paula Robertson, Rachel Hartell, Rebecca Leuw, Roberta Payton, Sandy Calico, Sarah Brough, Susan Gaszczak, Zoe Whitley Richmond.

A personal thank you to my webhost, TSOHost, Steve Bartholomew at curve21.com web design, Kim Johnson at Little Helper/FunPod, Sarah Mayer and Paula Figgett at Kaizo/Flip HD Video Camera, Hannah Groves at NEFF, GreenPan UK and Fuel/Salter UK.

Very special thank you to Laura Miller, my friend and producer of my radio show, Brett Spencer, Mark Norman, Nicki Wilson, Laurence Culhane, all the senior management, Jonathan Marsh and my colleagues at BBC Three Counties Radio for their invaluable support and guidance.

Most importantly I want to thank my family and friends who all mean the world to me. I can't thank everyone by name but I must thank four people individually: Jo, for being such an amazingly supportive wife and a remarkable mummy to Archie; my wonderful parents for their love and guidance; and my lovely sister, Juliet, for her constant stream of helpful ideas.

And of course… Archie! My funny, wilful, gorgeous little boy and ever-willing sous-chef. Thanks for joining me on this incredible ride. I hope that you will read this book in the future and be as proud of yourself as I am of you right now.

First published in Great Britain in 2011 by
Hodder & Stoughton

An Hachette UK company

1

ISBN 978 1 444 71371 8

Photography © Veronique Leplat
Design by Bobby Birchall, Bobby&Co
Typeset in Glypha
Printed and bound by Rotolito Lombarda Spa, Italy

Hodder & Stoughton policy is to use papers that are natural, renewable and recyclable products and made from wood grown in sustainable forests. The logging and manufacturing processes are expected to conform to the environmental regulations of the country of origin.

Hodder & Stoughton Ltd
338 Euston Road
London NW1 3BH

www.hodder.co.uk

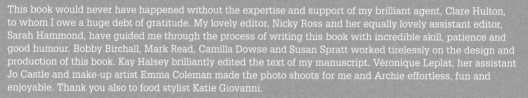